Long Road Home

Long Road Home

Testimony of a North Korean Camp Survivor

KIM YONG with KIM SUK-YOUNG

COLUMBIA UNIVERSITY PRESS  NEW YORK

Columbia University Press is grateful to the Committee for Human Rights in North Korea for permission to use satellite images produced by DigitalGlobe and Space Imaging Asia and printed in the Committee's 2003 report by David Hawk, "Hidden Gulag: Exposing North Korea's Prison Camps."

Columbia University Press
Publishers Since 1893
New York Chichester, West Sussex

Library of Congress Cataloging-in-Publication Data
Kim, Yong, 1950-.
Long road home : testimony of a North Korean camp survivor / Kim Yong with Kim Suk-Young.
p. cm.
Includes bibliographical references.
ISBN 978-0-231-14746-0 (cloth : alk. paper)
I. Kim, Yong, 1950- 2. Political prisoners—Korea (North)—Biography. 3. Concentration camps—Korea (North) 4. Forced labor—Korea (North) 5. Korea (North)—Social conditions. I. Kim, Suk-Young, 1970- II. Title.
HV9815.6.K56 2009
365.45092—dc22
[B]
2008044140

Columbia University Press books are printed on permanent and durable acid-free paper.
This book was printed on paper with recycled content.
Printed in the United States of America
c 10 9 8 7 6 5 4 3 2 1

Contents

Preface

I met Kim Yong for the first time in the fall of 2004, when I led a group of Dartmouth College undergraduate students to a human rights conference hosted by LiNK (Liberty in North Korea) at Cornell University. As a rare survivor of a North Korean penal labor camp, Kim Yong appeared on stage, frail but dignified, and began to speak of his experience, mostly unknown to the outside world. Kim Yong calmly narrated the rise and fall of his fortune in North Korea and the unspeakable sufferings he and many other North Koreans had to endure. But his story was also about having hope in places where death seemed more desirable than life. Kim Yong's face, still carrying the scars of torture and pain, first remained calm but soon was deluged as the throbbing memories turned into two rivulets of tears that kept flowing endlessly back to the sea of memories.

This book started to write itself from that moment. Following the conference, I maintained close contact with Kim Yong, which soon developed into friendship with occasional phone calls and face-to-face conversations. We started to have more frequent conversations after I moved from New Hampshire to California in the summer of 2005. In the fall of the same year, I had a chance to invite him to Santa Barbara for an extended series of interviews, which yielded approximately twenty hours of recordings. This book is primarily a translation of the direct transcripts of those interviews conducted in Korean, but more importantly, it is a witness to one of the gravest tragedies to have taken place in our time.

Presenting a powerful glimpse inside the secret world of the North Korean gulag system, *Long Road Home* is the story of Kim Yong, the only known prisoner to have survived the atrocious labor camp No. 14 in

Hamkyeong province, North Korea, otherwise completely secret from the outside world. Accused of being the son of an American spy, Kim spent six years working in a coal mine 2,400 feet underground, during which time he saw almost no sunlight. After months of meticulous planning, he made his dramatic escape by hiding in a coal train, which took him out of the camp. With help from old friends, he soon reached the border between North Korea and China. From there he went to Mongolia and eventually to South Korea. Kim came to the United States in 2003 and testified before the Human Rights Committee of the U.S. Congress, and his story has been featured by numerous international media outlets.

Kim's life was marked by drama from the beginning. When he was three years old, his father was executed as a spy for the United States. To save him from the collective guilt attributed to the families of political wrongdoers in North Korea, Kim's mother placed him in an orphanage under a false name. Without knowledge of this secret past, Kim grew up, entered the military, and eventually became a lieutenant colonel in the national security police. Like other military and security units and departments, his unit set up an income-gathering business, and Kim worked his way up to become a vice president in a trading company. As a foreign currency earner for the regime, he once submitted loyalty funds to Kim Jong-il, who in response sent a personal note promising to protect Kim's family. Kim Yong's high-flying career ironically came to an end when he was recommended for a promotion, upon which his real identity was discovered during a meticulous background clearance check.

Before his imprisonment, Kim had an imported car, a luxury unheard of for most, and freedom to travel anywhere in North Korea, another privilege unimaginable in a country where ordinary people need to obtain permission even for a brief trip. This gave Kim unusual opportunity to access various sectors of North Korean society. His encounters with corrupt party officials, Japanese trade partners, illegal prostitutes, privileged citizens of Pyongyang, impoverished rural farmers, victims of apocalyptic famine, subhuman camp guards, suffering political prisoners, and the various people he met during his dangerous escape make his testimony a rich and multifaceted saga. His story presents not only invaluable information about the violation of human rights but also detailed ethnographic records of the North Korean people's daily lives. While this book serves as one of the first narratives to provide a detailed account of life in the North Korean labor camps, it also captures a lively picture of North Korean people of all walks of life. Kim's epic journey from North Korea to the United States is a dignified testament to the power of the human spirit to overcome even the darkest forms of oppression, torture, and ideological terror.

As translator and transcriber, I constantly had to make decisions to capture accurately the unique array of Kim's experiences and bring them to life in English. Having grown up in South Korea in a relatively stable environment for most of my life, I had no firsthand experience of North Korea, let alone the extraordinary conditions Kim had to endure. Although Kim Yong and I share the same language and certain common grounds of Korean culture, and although we lived not too far away from each other—the distance between Pyongyang and Seoul being only 120 miles—we seem to have existed in parallel universes. When he was enjoying full success as a foreign currency–earning officer in the National Security Agency in North Korea, I was a high school student consumed by the prospect of the college entrance exam in the south. When he was suddenly arrested one morning in 1993, I was passionately flipping through thick Russian novels in college. When he was fighting for his life every minute in the labor camp in 1996, I had left home to pursue graduate studies in the United States. How was I to overcome the profound gap between us, marked by differences in age, gender, and finally the ideology that divided the two Koreas into hostile regimes? How were our perspectives supposed to merge and create a singular narrative?

In interviewing Kim Yong, I tried my best to learn not only *what* happened to him but also *how* these events unfolded and what they meant for him. In presenting his responses here, I have tried to balance facts with reflections, history with contemplation as much as possible. However, due to the vast time span covered in this book, and due to the emotional toll the interview process took on Kim Yong, I was often not able to go much beyond simple facts. Thus, when I started transcribing the recorded interviews, I had to make a conscious decision: how to negotiate between the commitment to faithfully capture Kim's cadence and voice and the impulse to embellish his story with literary flair. I discussed this very issue with Kim Yong many times, and we concluded that it would be best to transcribe Kim's story from the original interviews with minimal dramatization or stylistic alteration, which might diminish the credibility of his story. At the same time, we also felt the necessity to polish the raw narrative to make it more readable, so long as this process would not interfere with the veracity of the events presented. For this reason, readers may feel the stylistic platitude embedded in the narrative alternating with more literary trimming, since that is a specific choice I made as transcriber of Kim Yong's recorded narrative. The result is a narrative told in a straightforward but honest voice, interwoven with infrequent emotional reflections, that recounts the events as they happened to a man who suffered the unimaginable. This book is meant to be a memoir based on the first-person narrative, which is why I refrained from overwhelming intervention as a translator and transcriber. I do strongly believe in the power of Kim's original voice, with its minimal, unadorned style and simple integrity.

The stories told by Kim Yong in this book span over fifty years, almost coterminous with the history of North Korea itself. They touch upon almost all aspects of North Korean life, from everyday matters such as family relationships, schooling, and communal life to more national and transnational issues of political structure, economic crisis, migration, and infringement on human rights. I hope that reading it provides an occasion to visit these questions from the unique perspective of an individual who has lived through it all with remarkable dignity and resilience.

S. Y. Kim

Acknowledgments

We often think about the countless North Koreans who have disappeared. The ones whose names we don't know, the ones whose faces we can't recognize. But sometimes, we see them lying frozen by the riverbank in the thick of the winter night. At other times, we feel their pain as they gasp for their last breath, trying in vain to reignite the dying flame of life.

At those moments, we hear their voices whispering the names of loved ones.

Like always, their tears feel warm.

We wanted readers to think of them while reading this story, and may our thoughts ease their souls as they make their journey to the other world. This book is our humble dedication to their memories.

So many have taken part in making this story come to life. Support from colleagues and students at Dartmouth and UCSB was indispensable in finishing this project. A Burke Junior Faculty Fellowship from Dartmouth, an Academic Senate Travel Grant, a Hellman Family Junior Faculty Fellowship, an Interdisciplinary Humanitics Center Research Fellowship, and Performance Studies and East Asian Culture Research Focus Groups from UCSB made it possible for us to have an ongoing conversation. We would like to thank Columbia University Press for providing a home for this project, Jennifer Crewe for believing in our mission, Leslie Kriesel for skillful editing, and the two anonymous readers for their comments. Finally, we would like to thank our families, both dead and living. Y, B, J, Michael Berry, our parents, brothers, and sisters—we would be nothing without your love.

K.Y. and K.S.Y.

Author's Note

For transliteration of Korean words, I will consistently use the official Korean-language romanization system released by South Korea's Ministry of Culture and Tourism in 2000. However, for words well known in the English-speaking world, I will use the conventional transliteration instead of strictly applying the 2000 romanization system: hence "Pyongyang" instead of "Pyeoyang," "Kim Jong-il" instead of "Kim Jeong-il." In order to clarify the original pronunciation, I will separate syllables with hyphens when necessary.

Following the Korean convention, for all Korean names used in this book, family names precede personal names: hence "Kim Jong-il" instead of "Jong-il Kim." Kim Yong made it clear that he wishes to protect some individuals by using initials, not real names, to designate them.

Long Road Home

North Korea is a place of palpable contradictions. On the one hand, in the years immediately following the devastating Japanese colonial rule (1910–45) and the Korean War (1950–53), it achieved a remarkable degree of economic growth and social reconstruction. On the other hand, it has sustained its legitimacy through a ruthless dictatorship and personality cult that can only be maintained at the cost of forsaking civil society and human rights. According to North Korea's official claim, everyone lives a happy life, and yet, in recent years, so many have left this paradise in search of food and better chances for survival. In North Korea people live very closely with their family and neighbors in tightly knit communities, but at the same time, most fear to speak their minds freely, even to the closest members of their family. Amid these contradictions, Kim Yong lived a life marked by unexpected turns and impasses. Here he invites us to travel with him along the discursive unfolding of his fate.

Kim Yong's vicissitude directly reflects the historical scars modern Korea carries to this day. Born in 1950, the year the Korean War broke out, he tells a story that grew out of Korea's precarious realities in the aftermath of World War II, the subsequent partition, and the perpetuation of division throughout the Cold War era. Korea was a Japanese colony from 1910 to 1945, and when Japan surrendered to the Allied Forces in the final days of the Pacific War, Koreans rejoiced at the prospect of establishing an independent state. However, despite this unanimous desire to become a sovereign nation, Korean society was anything but a monolithic entity in 1945. Emerging from the long period of colonial rule by a nation that many Koreans disparage as culturally inferior, Korea in 1945 consisted of motley segments of social groups who held varying interests and colliding ideals about their future as an independent postcolonial nation. This variegated social spectrum could be best described as two opposing ideological camps with the vast majority of Koreans in the ambiguous area situated in the middle. Carter Eckert and other historians have detailed this polarized makeup of postcolonial Korean society in the following terms:

> To the right of the line were the majority of propertied and educated Koreans, many of whom had cooperated in one way or another with the colonial regime. Most were resistant to social changes such as land reform. Others, including some of the more progressive landlords who had transferred a portion of their assets into industry, regarded change as inevitable, but were anxious to control and contain it so as to preserve their privileged positions in the society. Also on the right were those Koreans with less education and little or no property who had faithfully served the Japanese state, such as the Koreans who comprised about forty percent of the colonial police force. On the left side of the spectrum were Koreans of varying backgrounds, including students, intellectuals, peasants, and workers who had been politicized by the colonial experience. Some were actual members of the Communist Party or felt an affinity toward communism as a force that had opposed Japanese rule and advocated justice for the poor and oppressed. All were committed first to a thorough purge of collaborators from positions of power and influence. They sought, in addition, some form of redistribution of wealth, such as land reform, that would redress the inequities of the past and transform Korea into a more egalitarian society.[1]

The division of Korea was not only a geographic division by the Allied forces along the 38th parallel but also an internal stratification among Koreans. Although this social divide might have been typical of any postcolonial state that emerged after World War II, what set postcolonial Korea apart was its unfortunate geopolitical proximity to the center of shifting power dynamics between the United States and the Soviet

Union at the dawn of the Cold War. The tension between the two forces that occupied the Korean peninsula escalated, but Koreans, despite their diverse class and political affiliations, shared a strong common desire to establish an undivided nation. That desire was met with challenges posed by the Allied forces, which set out to address the messy legacies left by thirty-six years of Japan's colonial rule over Korea—most significantly, to disarm a significant number of Imperial Army troops left in Korean territory when Japan surrendered in August 1945. The United States and the Soviet Union divided the task by separating Korea into two halves along the 38th parallel; the north was entrusted to the Soviet Union and the south to the United States.

The division into two Koreas was anything but the Korean people's own desire. As Gregory Henderson, a former U.S. Foreign Service officer, noted: "No division of a nation in the present world is so astonishing in its origin as the division of Korea; none is so unrelated to conditions or sentiment within the nation itself at the time the division was effected; none is to this day so unexplained."[2] The 38th parallel was supposed to serve as a temporary border separating two zones of bilateral trusteeship in Korea. But as Cold War politics dominated the dynamics of the inter-Korean relationship, the 38th parallel became the border between two hostile regimes, North and South Korea. In 1948, each held its own elections and subsequently established a separate government, turning what started out as a temporary line into an impermeable wall that blocked the free movement of people and ideology. The two regimes collided in a tragic civil war that claimed millions of lives on both sides before being brought to a halt through armistice in 1953. The 38th parallel still functions as a rigid border in the post–Korean War era.

What complicated the internal politics of partitioned Korea was the fact that the division imposed by the outside forces did not symmetrically separate the political left and right into North and South Korea, but arbitrarily created two sides composed of discursive groups with varying interests and backgrounds. After the 1945 partition and especially after the end of the Korean War in 1953, there still remained pockets of resistance within each regime—most notably, leftist communist sympathizers in the south and antirevolutionaries, including landlords and former collaborators of Japan and America, in the north—all to be brutally suppressed by the regimes led by the pro-American Li Seung-man in the south and the Soviet-backed Kim Il-sung in the north. The large population in the middle with neither political interest nor clearly defined positions was eventually forced to follow the ideological orientation of the respective regimes. It was under these circumstances that Kim Yong's father became trapped on the wrong side of the border in the aftermath of the Korean War. Having worked as an informant for the American troops and the South Korean army and thereby contributed to the North Korean forces' arrest during the war, Kim Yong's father belonged to the poisonous segment of collaborators with foreign imperialists in the north. He thus earned arguably the worst kind of "antirevolutionary" label in North Korean society—a stigma so formidable that it would even doom the following generation.

Given how brutally North Korea suppressed any collaborators of its sworn enemies—South Korea, Japan, and America—it would have been much better for Kim's father and his family to have ended up south of the border. This, of course, is an observation with a benefit of hindsight; amid the three years of chaotic war, who could have known that the division of Korea would only be strengthened for more than half a century? From the end of the Korean War up to the present moment,[3] both Koreas have prohibited their citizens from engaging in any level of humanitarian contact outside of government-controlled channels, such as communications between separated family members, intellectual and cultural exchanges, and any type of political discourse. Unfortunately, in the process of creating two ideologically and politically hostile regimes out of one homogenous nation, the division of Korea was hardened into a structure that has perpetuated the rituals of the Cold War and regulates every aspect of life in both parts.[4] Free discussion of the other side—unless it took the form of fierce anti–South or North Korean propaganda—was unthinkable for Koreans.

Thus, the foundation of the North Korean state itself was predicated on the illegitimacy of the other side, South Korea, perceived as a puppet state obsequiously bowing to the evil Japanese and American imperialists and compromising the dignity of the Korean people. In comparison, North Korea founded its legitimacy as the righteous Korean state upon nationalistic ideals of self-reliance. Based on the close reading of materials that recently became available at the U.S. National Archives and Records Administration, Bruce Cumings suggests that, unlike many assumed, North Korea was far from being a typical Soviet puppet state:

> The closest comparisons to North Korea were Romania and Yugoslavia—not the states under complete Soviet hegemony, such as East Germany. . . . Soviet influence competed with Chinese influence, and both conflicted with indigenous political forms and practices. The Democratic Republic of Korea (DPRK) was and is a divergent case among postwar Marxist-Leninist systems, representing a profound reassertion of native Korean political practice—from the superordinate role of the leader to his self-reliant ideology, to the Hermit Kingdom foreign policy.[5]

The unique path that has emerged in the north has deep roots in a Korean brand of nationalism that puts much emphasis on racial purity and the nation as a tightly controlled patriarchal family. Such a strong focus on ethnocentric nationalism, after all, is not too different from the approach taken in the south. Using this nationalist directive coupled with progressive socialist reforms, North Korea was able to undertake popular reforms such as the collectivization of land and the institutionalization of mandatory primary education.

To a certain degree, the newborn North Korean state in the early years was faithful to these collective ideals as it made noteworthy progress, fueled by the enthusiasm of its people, the charismatic leadership of Kim Il-sung, and generous aid from the Soviet Union and the People's Republic of China. In the first decade following its establishment, North Korea was a place brimming with energy and ambition led by Kim Il-sung, who had spent his formative years in Manchuria fighting the Japanese imperial army in a guerrilla squad and then in the People's Liberation Army as well as the Soviet Army, before returning to liberated Korea in 1945. North Koreans, even the majority of defectors who voluntarily left, still revere Kim Il-sung as the only legitimate leader of the independent Korean nation and the father who genuinely cared for his people. Even after his death in 1994, he still inspires awe and respect from North Korean people who look to his governance as the golden days gone by. We see the same kind of deep and sincere affection felt by Kim Yong for the Great Leader, from his childhood until his arrest.

As much as Kim Il-sung was loved by the North Korean people, he was equally ambitious and ruthless in consolidating his power. On the domestic front, he achieved this end through brutal purges of his political enemies that terrorized many, including his closest allies. One of the most visible targets to emerge in the process was those who had assisted Japanese imperialists and Americans during Japanese colonial rule and the subsequent Korean War. To have a father labeled as an American spy was to have a death sentence in the North Korean context, and it was under these conditions that Kim Yong's mother decided to disguise him as a war orphan and place him in a state-run orphanage to guarantee him a better future.

A state-run orphanage might not conjure up a happy picture in readers' minds, but in North Korea, the situation was somewhat different in the 1950s. One of the ways North Korea attempted to invent itself as socialist paradise was through the humane treatment of orphans who had lost their parents during Japanese colonial rule and the Korean War. There are numerous narratives about how the national father Kim Il-sung treated war orphans as if they were his own children. Countless propaganda paintings and posters featuring Kim Il-sung greeting war orphans in tattered clothes and bare feet and welcoming them into his red-carpeted office adorn print media and public spaces. By all accounts, these propaganda efforts seem to have emerged out of the North Korean state's sincere desire to provide for the orphans. As Kim Yong's narrative recounts, they were even sent to orphanages in other socialist countries on exchange programs in order to testify not only to their homeland's growing socialist friendship but also to North Korea's successful care of the most vulnerable members of its society. As we learn from Kim Yong's testimony, Kim Il-sung must have genuinely felt for war orphans, so much so that he even instructed party leaders to adopt them and provide for them equally as their own children—a directive that was faithfully followed by Kim Yong's adoptive parents and profoundly shaped Kim's future.

Not only war orphans but also North Korean children in general were treated as important members of society. Until the devastating famine in the 1990s , by all indications, children in North Korea were regarded with love and care as long as their family members had the proper class background, such as anti-Japanese guerrilla fighters during the colonial period, impoverished peasants, workers, soldiers, and war martyrs. As Helen-Louise Hunter argues, "parents dote on their children no less than parents anywhere else in the world. In fact, if anything, they seem to live for their children, perhaps because their own lives offer little but hope for a better future for their children. Parents make sacrifices gladly, saving as much as they can all during their lives to secure the best for their children."[6] For a brief period, Kim Yong also had lavish pampering by his adoptive parents, but it should be emphasized that his life in this adoptive family represents a very small fraction of childhood experience in North Korea. The power and privilege his adoptive parents enjoyed cannot be viewed as a general condition of families residing in Pyongyang, let alone those living in the rural areas.

One measure to understand the extraordinary nature of Kim Yong's privilege after adoption is Mangyeongdae Children's Palace (*Mangyeongdae sonyeon gungjeon*), where he was sent to practice judo. This place grooms talented children with superb class background in all areas of the arts and sports under the tutelage of first-rate instructors. Some learn to perfect their musical skills while others learn how to dance. The Mangyeongdae Children's Palace arts program is so reputed that it is a must stop for visiting foreign dignitaries, who are treated to impeccable talent shows staged by the young North Korean students. It was there that the boy Kim Yong made the acquaintance of the elder sister of Go Yeonghee, Kim Jong-il's third wife-to-be, whose sons are nowadays expected to become the successors of Kim Jong-il. In a color-illustrated handbook for foreign tourists published in English by the National Tourism Administration in 2002, Mangyeongdae Children's Palace is described with exuberant national pride:

> It is an extracurricular educational institution for the school children in Pyongyang. The palace was built thanks to the loving care of President **Kim Il Sung** [*sic*] and General **Kim Jong Il** [*sic*] who have regarded children as the kings of the country. The palace has floor space of 103,000 square metres and covers an area of 300,000 square metres. A sculptural group is in front of the palace. The central hall runs high through to the third floor, links several sections of the palace and is decorated with 19.5-metre high marble pillars and 2.5 ton heavy chandelier. On both sides of the central hall 36-metre long large lily-of-the-valley pattern chandeliers run from the first floor through to the 6th floor. The palace consists of the science hall, gymnasium, art hall, and swimming pool, over 200 circle rooms and activity rooms and a 2000-seat theatre with an automatic stage. Every day more than 5,000 schoolchildren conduct various extracurricular activities in the palace.[7]

Such excessive opulence, truly deserving the appellation of "palace," was partly designed to create a social network for the future elites of North Korean society. As a member of this high circle, Kim Yong continued his privileged life into adulthood, marrying a political educator with a good revolutionary background and landing a preferred position as a foreign currency–earning officer in the National Security Agency. This chapter in Kim Yong's life is arguably one of the most extraordinary, as his job, to earn foreign currency by conducting off-the-record trade with neighboring countries such as Japan and Russia, not only escalated his high-flying career but also provides a glimpse of a very obscure brand of North Korean capitalism. With a few exceptions,[8] little has been documented about North Korea's government-led enterprise to earn foreign currency. According to Kim Yong, the primary purpose of setting up a foreign currency–earning department in almost every major government agency was to provide the North Korean leaders with hard currency. These departments were operating according to the strictest rules of the market economy, where generating profit is the primary goal and the survival of the fittest forces necessary mergers and acquisitions of ill-performing departments. With this fascinating view of how the underworld economy designed to serve a few leaders' wealth directly contradicted the official political philosophy of serving the community, it is difficult to fathom how pervasively this off-the-record system transformed North Korean society and how it might have influenced the recent emergence of limited market economy. However, it would not be far-fetched to assume that the often-reported North Korean embassies' illegal activities on foreign soil, such as drug smuggling, arms sales, and counterfeiting foreign currency, are the descendants of the practice of using government agencies to generate profit for the leaders as recounted by Kim Yong.[9]

Kim Yong worked hard to reach a leadership position in this trading company, and in return, he enjoyed access to material goods and access to the outside world. Such privileges cannot be shared by all members of the society. Although North Korea is supposedly a classless socialist state, it has reinforced class divisions as formidably as the premodern society with its caste system did in the past. North Koreans regard *seongbun*, or, roughly translated, "socioeconomic or class background,"[10] as the primary factor in one's future prospects. *Seongbun* is predetermined by family background, and there is nothing an individual can do to improve it.

Without good *seongbun*, individual talent stands for nothing. As Charles Armstrong points out:

> Social stratification had been one of the most enduring characteristics of Korean society before the twentieth century. . . . Rather than push for the elimination of social distinction at first, the emerging North Korean regime attempted to make social categories *more* explicit by carefully recording the social stratum (*seongbun*) of each individual. . . . The result of the North Korean revolution . . . was not the elimination of social hierarchy as such, but a radical change in the *content* of hierarchy.[11]

Indeed, the extent to which such social stratification regulated people's lives was absolutely unchallengeable, so much so that Kim Yong's mother took the drastic measure of falsifying the birth background of her two sons, who would have incomparably brighter futures as war orphans than as the sons of an American spy. As Hunter comments: "It is very difficult to improve one's *seongbun*, however, particularly if the stigma derives from the pre-Revolutionary class status or behavior of one's parents or relatives."[12] Considering that the Korean Workers' Party (*Joseon rodongdang*), arguably one of the most formidable social organizations in North Korea, keeps a detailed record of individuals' *seongbun* with regular updates, we can fathom the grave risk Kim's mother took out of sheer desperation. It is quite obvious that had she and her family, with such incorrigible background, had freedom to leave North Korea, they would have done so. But most Koreans, even now, have neither the freedom to choose which Korea they want to live in nor the mobility to visit the other side without heavy surveillance from both states.

Casting a sideways glance at other socialist states, we find practices similar to the North Korean *seongbun*, which marked undesired social groups and stigmatized them permanently in the aftermath of the socialist revolution. Richard K. Carton notes that "every Communist assumption of power—in Poland, Czechoslovakia, Hungary, Romania, Bulgaria, Yugoslavia, and Albania—was accompanied by mass arrests aimed primarily at the elimination of the opposition. Some prisoners were interned and others were assigned to forced labor."[13] Likewise, in the People's Republic of China, as Philip F. Williams and Yenna Wu's study shows, a similar process of grouping undesirable people took place on a massive scale: "Justification of large-scale political arrests . . . would recur in the legal policies of and criminal law instituted by successive Chinese Communist regimes throughout the twentieth century. This general pattern was much the same for Leninist regimes throughout Eurasia, especially during the phase of consolidation."[14] What is intriguing about this effort at massive elimination of certain social classes, however, is not only the creation of the so-called antirevolutionary class but also the fact that most of the antirevolutionaries ended up being absorbed by the state as a source of free labor. As Williams and Yu argue, "Because of their bad class background and the government's need for cheap labor, able-bodied rich farmers and landlords who were charged with no crime at all were also often conscripted for coercive service in the hard labor brigades."[15]

The political cleansing of class enemies obviously had repercussions in the economic sphere across the socialist states, but the question of how the North Korean purge of antirevolutionaries became linked to the government's economic policy has not yet been fully investigated. According to Kim Yong's account, the North Korean prisoners provided more than twelve hours of labor a day, which makes it reasonable to assume that the state must have reaped a handsome profit from their forced labor. And yet, the degree of near-death starvation that the prisoners experienced would have limited their productivity, so it is difficult to imagine any significant revenue being generated in such a devastating environment. The driving force that created the penal labor camp system in North Korea seems to have been political rather than economic. Kim Yong was generating significant profit in foreign currency for the government before his arrest, and keeping him in that position would have been much more useful for Kim Jong-il's financial needs than sending him to the mining camp, where nearly dead prisoners worked much slower than normal workers. The labor camps introduced in Kim's testimony are extermination camps where purging the antirevolutionary elements of the society must have been the primary purpose.

Kwanliso, simply referred to as "labor camps"[16] or "camps" in this book, occupy a special place in North Korean life. Located in secluded areas, each contains between 5,000 and 50,000 prisoners, totaling perhaps some 150,000 to 200,000 prisoners throughout North Korea, according to David Hawk's report for the U.S. Committee for Human Rights in North Korea.[17] However, what seems more significant about the camps is the horror they conjure up in the minds of the people and their symbolic function in disciplining the behavior of North Koreans in society. North Korean people know too well that once labeled as anti-revolutionary, they will be sent to the labor camps "without any judicial process or legal recourse whatsoever, for lifetime sentences of extremely hard labor in mining, timber-cutting, or farming enterprise,"[18] and that "the prisoners live under brutal conditions in permanent situations of deliberately contrived semi-starvation."[19]

Kim Yong's narrative provides a unique glimpse into two different camp sites, No. 14 and No. 18, where he was detained. He is the only person known to have walked out alive from No. 14 and the only one to have successfully escaped No. 18 to tell the details of conditions at these facilities. His testimonies are invaluable: without his willingness to share his experience, these clandestine sites would have been unknown to the outside world.[20] Of all the harrowing accounts regarding labor camps, the most disturbing arguably is the torment of near-death starvation to which inmates are subject while forced to do more than twelve hours of backbreaking labor every day. According to Kim Yong, the daily food ration in No. 14 and No. 18 consisted of three handfuls of corn kernels accompanied by a little rough salt and a bowl of watery soup—a portion deliberately designed to starve inmates to slow and excruciating death.

The extreme conditions at the North Korean labor camps become clear when we compare them to the food-rationing systems in political prisons of other socialist countries. To provide but one example, the early Soviet labor camps in 1935 rationed meager portions of food, but when compared to the testimonies of the North Korean camp survivors,[21] the Soviet ration described in the following passage comes across as a rather sumptuous feast:

> According to norms adopted in December 1935, camp prisoners daily received at least 400 grams of rye bread, along with hot dishes for breakfast and lunch. Approximate guidelines for food preparation called for 15 grams of flour per person per day, 60–80 grams of groats, and 500 grams of vegetables. Fish (160–80 grams) was served twenty-two times per month, and meat (70 grams), eight times per month. Prisoners received 350–400 grams of sugar per month. In theory, this meager ration could be increased if the work tasks were completed.[22]

The Soviet inmates, as was the case with their PRC counterparts, could also receive food parcels from family members, although there was a strict regulation as to how much they could get each time. According to Williams and Yu's research, the Chinese camp inmates could receive no more than one parcel per month, the weight of limited to five kilograms or so.[23] Such food parcels sent by family members are unknown to North Korean camp prisoners.

The extreme food rationing in labor camps must have been exacerbated by the deadly famine that swept across North Korea in the 1990s. The failure of the state-engineered food distribution system, coupled with natural disasters in 1994–95, devastated the countryside where most prison camps were located. Stephen Haggard and Marcus Noland's recent study tells us that this apocalyptic event, claiming up to one million lives, "ranks as one of the most destructive of the twentieth century."[24] It was a man-made disaster stemming from the combination of the central government's poor decision making and systemic failure rather than from natural calamity.

> Slow to respond to crisis—as closed, authoritarian governments so frequently are—the government not only limited effective targeting, monitoring, and assessment of humanitarian assistance, but cut off whole portions of the country from desperately needed help just as the famine was cresting. These government actions—and failure to act—are not incidental to the famine and ongoing food shortages; they are central to any explanation of it. The state's culpability in this vast misery elevates the North Korean famine to a crime against humanity.[25]

There is no doubt that the difficulties endured by the North Korean people in the 1990s were even worse in labor camps, but the famine testifies to the harrowing reality that the conditions in the labor camps and "normal" society were not that different; perhaps the variation was in the degree of hardship rather than its nature.

Ironically, it was this lethal famine that facilitated Kim's escape across North Korea to China. As Kim tells us, the famine in the late 1980s and early 1990s, when the central food distribution system collapsed, triggered a massive mobilization of starving people, forced to travel around in search of food. Whereas civilians had needed permission to travel in the past, by the time Kim escaped from the camp in 1998, the central government found it virtually impossible to prevent starving economic migrants from moving around the country, and at times, even outside the country in search of means of survival. The journey Kim Yong made across the Chinese border is typical of many North Korean economic migrants and defectors who still desperately seek asylum. Even today, an undocumented number of North Koreans, who have endured monumental suffering for the past fifteen years or so, continue to escape their homeland, often crossing the border to China taking the same risky route that Kim once followed. Kim Yong's story is an ongoing story, and his destiny is shared by countless other Koreans.

The fate of these border crossers—estimated from under 100,000 to 400,000, according to varying sources[26]—is precarious and their future obscure at best once theyreach China. Even in the face of the international community's persistent requests, China still does not recognize North Korean border crossers as international refugees, which poses enormous challenges for NGOs and other organizations intent on helping these North Koreans reach a safe place. Although the North Korean Human Rights Bill passed the U.S. Congress in October 2004, concrete measures to assist North Korean refugees have yet to be implemented, leaving the fate of these stateless and undocumented border crossers mostly to a few NGOs. It cannot be overemphasized that there needs to be a systematic agreement at the state level, involving international organizations, such as the United Nations Higher Commission for Refugees, to guarantee basic human rights to the increasing number of North Korean refugees in China and elsewhere before they reach a safe haven. Kim Yong was fortunate enough to fall under the protection of South Korean Christian missionaries who led him through his journey. But not all refugees are so lucky. Arguably the worst kind of disaster that can happen to North Korean border crossers in China is sexual trafficking of women. North Korean women who do not have legal status in China often find themselves forced into sexual slavery or are sold into rural families as brides for Chinese males who otherwise cannot afford to find mates.[27] The harsh fate awaiting North Korean border crossers remains underdocumented at best, and international efforts are needed to end this humanitarian crisis.

The high socialist ideals set up in the early North Korean state have degenerated into gruesome reality and erupted as crisis, to the point where the government cannot even provide the basic means for survival for its people, let alone a utopian life in a socialist paradise. This crisis by no means haunts North Korea alone—it also falls on every nation's conscience, as human rights infringement and politico-economic migration can only be understood through a transnational scope. In this respect, while Kim Yong's stories primarily read as a chronicle of the North Korean nation's failure, they also capture a broader predicament with which mankind has been struggling throughout history. Only the future will tell whether such drastic failure to protect its people will lead to the downfall of the North Korean state. In the meantime, we can only fathom the depth of this national and transnational tragedy unfolding in the present tense through Kim's haunting stories.

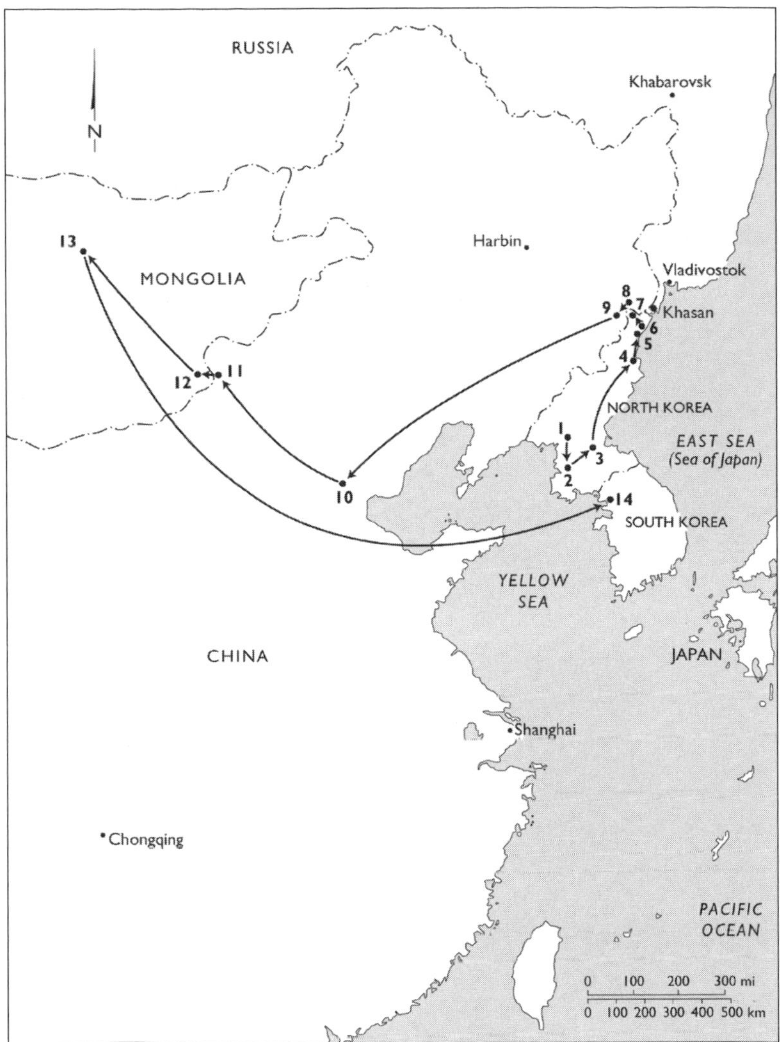

Kim Yong's Escape Route

1. Bukchang
2. West Pyongyang Station
3. Go-on
4. Cheongjin
5. Rajin
6. Unggi
7. Namyang
8. Tumen
9. Yanji
10. Beijing
11. Erenhot
12. Dzamïn Üüd
13. Ulaanbaatar
14. Seoul

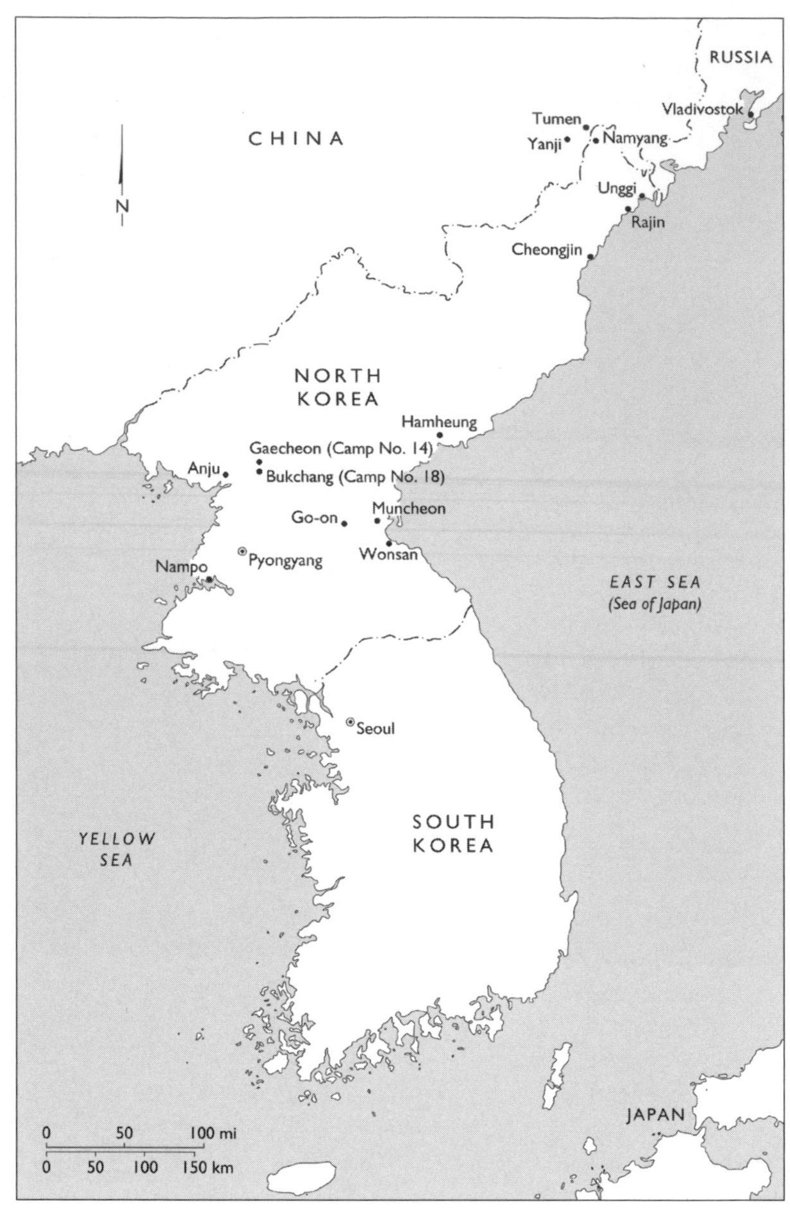
RUSSIA
Vladivostok
Tumen
Yanji
Namyang
CHINA
N
Unggi
Rajin
Cheongjin
NORTH
KOREA
Hamheung
Gaecheon (Camp No. 14)
Anju
Bukchang (Camp No. 18)
Muncheon
Go-on
Wonsan
Pyongyang
Nampo
EAST SEA
(Sea of Japan)
Seoul
SOUTH
KOREA
YELLOW
SEA
JAPAN
0 50 100 mi
0 50 100 150 km

Map of Korea

Rustling waves approach the shore in endless succession, damping the tips of my toes and luring my sight back to the horizon. Beyond that horizon lies a place I once called home. But on this side of the ocean, the shoreline appears etched with motley traces of strangers. When touched by the sea, they gradually melt as if they never existed. As I watch this rhythmic but futile movement, the shores of my heart, also marred by scars of memories, wells up with longing. But just like the infinitely shattered sand cannot hold back the waves, my fragmented being cannot contain the swaying memories.

Los Angeles, California. 2008.

The sun in the sky is melting from its own brilliance.

I close my eyes to rest, but myriads of faces appear even when my eyes see nothing, soon to dissolve into obscure figures. Long-forgotten names, the faint smell of my young children, the low voice of my wife, the wind blowing from bleak mountains, slowly moving trains, an endless journey through the night . . . where have they all gone?

I come from thousands of miles away. I am a stranger from a strange land, a restless specter in search of shelter. I've crossed the river in the netherworld and seen pillars of fire in the desert. Constantly longing for home, I wander around, accompanied by a long shadow cast from afar. I call out the names of once close friends, but hear nothing in return. I whisper the names of my wife and children, but they are simply a disappearing impression or warm and brief sensation, momentarily illuminating my presence, only to leave me behind in this strange world.

I grab a handful of sand and try to feel its warmth. But only dust remains on my palms—a silent reminder of the home I left for good. This emptiness makes me think of the strangers who must be living in my old home in Pyongyang. They must be strolling in the small garden my wife once cared for, but would they be aware of the previous residents whose lives were shattered into a thousand pieces? Would I recognize my home even if I were to return?

Home is an illusion.

An incorrigible wanderer who cannot avoid recurring nightmares, I drift from shore to shore.

Coming of Age 1

First Memories

But where was my home anyway?

What does my memory tell me about it?

My first home was the state-run orphanage in Pyongyang, where I grew up under the loving care of the Great Leader Kim Il-sung, the founding father of North Korea. My first dear memory about this home, however, is not associated with the Great Leader but with Kim Hye-hwa, the kind nanny who nurtured me even before I could remember. A warm, loving person, Kim Hye-hwa always had a modest but kind aura. This graceful lady had lost an infant son of my age during the Korean War, which added a tone of sadness to everything she did. I wondered whether I was the first baby orphan she took to breast-feed after the loss of her own child. Did I resemble him? I never asked, but she must have hoped to forget the dreadful void left in her when she took me in her arms.

Unlike Kim Hye-hwa, the other nannies were quite strict and severe in their treatment of orphans. Most nannies were either spinsters or widows who had lost their potential mates or husbands during the Korean War. As I recall, most of them unhappily realized that they were doomed to spend their entire life in an extended family of orphans, without male companions. They were absolutely unforgiving in punishing mischievous pranksters. Most of them were ready and willing to smack orphans when they misbehaved, or punish them by refusing to change diapers or feed them snacks. When it came to inculcating revolutionary ideology in us, however, the nannies transformed into dignified priestesses guarding the holy shrine of the living god Kim Il-sung.

> The sky is blue and I feel happy,
> Play the accordion out loud.
> I love my homeland, everyone lives happily,
> Our father, the Great Leader Kim Il-sung,
> The warm embrace of our party!

The lyrics of this first song I learned to sing made me happy, and inspired hope and trust in the hearts of the neglected orphans. I remember how my little body used to shudder with delight when I sang out the words "warm embrace," and how I longed for it every moment. Warm embrace. The party. Warm embrace. We are happy. Our Great Leader.

The nannies told us about our Great Leader's heroic revolutionary conquests. Naturally, the first sentence I learned to write was "Thank you, Great Leader Kim Il-sung." While listening to the revolutionary saga, we orphans were all mesmerized by his strong and handsome appearance. Accompanying this hero was the beautiful and courageous wife, Kim Jeong-suk,[1] who assisted Kim Il-sung's revolutionary projects with unflinching courage and self-sacrifice. Looking back, never did I doubt that the Kims were invincible gods who single-handedly rescued our homeland from the Japanese colonialists and American imperialists. They presided over our daily lives, looking down at us from the portraits hanging on the walls. Kim Il-sung's and Kim Jeong-suk's birthdays—April 15 and December 24 respectively—were memorable holidays, as abundant food and lavish presents were sent to us by the Korean Workers' Party (*Joseon rodongdang*). Male orphans collectively celebrated their unknown birthdays on the national mother Kim Jeong-suk's birthday, whereas female orphans celebrated theirs on the national father Kim Il-sung's birthday.

After the establishment of the socialist regime, the North Korean government confiscated the wealth of the landlords and capitalists and converted their properties into state facilities. The orphanage where I grew up, I was told, had been a wealthy landlord's mansion before the founding of North Korea. However, all the extravagant traces of the feudal past were replaced by revolutionary paraphernalia. The red flag of the Korean Workers' Party covered the walls where once must have stood panels displaying literati calligraphy; portraits of Kim Il-sung must have replaced delicate ink painting featuring flowers and butterflies on silk. I still remember that a stream flowed by the orphanage. Our nannies used it to wash everything that needed to be washed—rice, vegetables, clothes, and dirty orphans. The generous stream always provided for us without demanding anything in return. I would spend hours gazing at the water, fixated on the constant clear stream. When I stood in front of that eternal stillness in movement, the flow eventually stirred up my uneasiness and my questions, which merged with the current. I wasn't sure where they came from and where they were headed.

Who am I?

Where do I come from?

What will my future bring?

The stream always remained silent.

Like every child in North Korea, I learned eating habits shaped by daily political rituals. Each time the nannies handed out food, they told us that it came from the Great General Kim Il-sung. We would bow deeply in front of his portrait and thank him even before touching the food. Whenever I raised my head, the Great Leader was there in the photo, generously smiling, presiding over the children who eagerly prepared to eat.

Just like we were tutored to appreciate the Great Leader for everything we received, we were equally clear about whom we should hate for all the things we were deprived of. The nannies raised the orphans to believe that all class enemies of the laboring people—landlords and capitalists—were potbellied swine, who exploited poor people and gorged on too much food themselves without thinking of others. We took this lesson to heart and began to blame the class enemies for everything—including the absence of our parents. One day, a man with a rosy complexion and a huge belly visited our orphanage. This was Choi Yeong-gon, then the Vice-Premier of North Korea, who displayed the natural signs of a privileged man—his well-fed complexion beaming in a bright rosy shimmer while his heavy gait carried along his bulging belly. The grandee, however, ended up suffering at the hands of us vicious children. As soon as he entered the orphanage, he was attacked by the indignant orphans throwing stones and shouting out at the top of their full-blown lungs: "Away with the potbellied landlord, away with the greedy capitalist, away with the exploiter of the people!" As the embarrassed nannies were running around to stop their well-trained disciples, the generous vice-premier praised the children for their feisty revolutionary spirit with an embarrassed smile on his ruddy face.

Oh, how we hated the enemies with all our might!

Among those enemies we hated, Americans were at the top of the list.

Upon entering elementary school, we orphans were treated to an excursion to the American Imperial Massacre Remembrance Museum in Shincheon. We were told that this was where American soldiers massacred some 900 villagers, many of whom were women and children. The American troops led the defenseless civilians into an air raid shelter and locked them up. They spent three days in fear, not having a clue about what would happen to them. On the third day, the soldiers set the building on fire and burned everyone to death. The museum was a solemn place commemorating the victims of the atrocities committed by the American army during the Korean War. But more importantly, it was a place where we were reminded why we should hate America. The museum displayed the American commander's words directing the massacre. I visited this site so many times, even into my middle school days on school excursions, that I still remember every single line of the enemy commander's order: "My command is law. Kill everyone mercilessly, old or young. Your hands should not tremble." We were told that the American soldiers had separated children from mothers and burned them separately in ammunition storage facilities up the mountain. We were brought into a mausoleum and shown the walls where the victims' nails were embedded as they desperately gasped their last and wrote on the wall: "Avenge our death," and "Americans are our arch-enemies." The excursion guide also pointed out that the white layer on the wall was grease produced by incinerated human bodies. We were told that only orphans were given the opportunity to see the walls because allowing too many people to the site would inevitably bring too much air and sunlight to destroy the layer of grease. As one of the few privileged witnesses to the heinous acts done by the American imperialists, I shuddered at the sight. Everyone felt that if it weren't for our Great Father Kim Il-sung's courageous leadership, all of us would still be under the yoke of foreign domination. We all felt that the intense hatred for Americans soon transformed into equally intense love for our father. Our hearts and minds welled up with admiration for he who presided over the safety and dignity of our homeland.

Overall, war orphans were treated well because they were seen as the children of martyrs who had sacrificed themselves in defending the homeland. The state made sure that only children with excellent class background, from the households of soldiers, workers, and landless farmers, were admitted to orphanages. One day, a close friend of mine was picked up by his birth mother. All the orphans were so envious of him, but much later in life, I had the misfortune of encountering him at a penal labor camp. He told me that as soon as his mother brought him home from the orphanage, his entire family was sent to a camp. The only crime they had committed was to have a bad class background: they had been landlords during Japanese colonial rule. His mother presaged the impending family misfortune and wanted to protect him by disguising her son as an orphan, but her desperate plan was unfortunately short-lived.

The orphanage was not always a safe place, even for those fully grown. I remember there was a twenty-five-year-old orphan in my class, which was made up mostly of nine-year-olds. He ended up in the orphanage as a teenager after the war and idled away without finding either adoptive parents or a vocation. He might have been slightly retarded, which is why nobody adopted him until he turned older than even some of our nannies. He used to vent his frustration by slapping the little ones around at will. Large as he was, he had many enemies and virtually no supporters. So one day, the small ones, including myself, put our heads together and waited for him to enter the classroom, then threw a blanket over the giant so as to knock him down with our little fists. The lonely monster moaned while his chubby arms and legs helplessly reached out to resist. We moved collectively to bring down the enemy and triumphed—as if to prove the revolutionary lesson we had been taught about how little people can triumph over the strong enemy if they move as one family.

Although fierce revolutionaries at heart, we orphans were never shy of troublemaking. Each one quickly learned how to fight for his or her interests, which sometimes entailed forming groups representing similar background and interests to dominate other groups. In the 1950s, North Korea sent groups of orphans abroad to the communist countries, such as China and Romania, as a gesture of friendship consolidating international socialism. Korean orphans who spent some time abroad were extremely arrogant when they returned home. Puffed with attitude and a sense of superiority, they formed exclusive circles, admitting only their own. I was particularly envious of those who had spent some time in

China, because each of them had a glimmering golden-colored ballpoint pen with a shining miniature globe dangling from the end. Whenever those China-sent orphans detected envious gazes of admirers, they would brag about how the Chinese authorities presented them with those beautiful gifts and shook their hands upon their return to North Korea. The domestic orphans, including myself, painfully coveted the magically shimmering colors of their precious possessions. Nothing else, it seemed, was more prized and exotic than those pens. In order to conceal our envy, we gave the Chinese faction a tough time by constantly pestering them to fight. Despite our nannies' tear-inducing corporeal punishments, there were constant battles between "the Romanian faction" and "the Chinese faction" as well as between "the indigenous Koreans" and "the foreign faction."

But on rare occasions, orphans would truly unite. Children from our orphanage sometimes went for track meets where we would compete with children from other schools or day-care centers, playing soccer and running races. When the parents of those children cheered for their kids, my heart would ache with immeasurable sorrow and my entire body would feel pain. Whenever I heard parents' voices calling out the names of our competitors, my legs would lose all power and yield to those whose faces were happily beaming. Mommies and daddies were behind those little pricks! Mommies and daddies . . . there simply was no way I could ever compete with the attention and love they got. Nothing was more painful than to realize that we orphans did not have anyone to cheer for us. The pain then would easily turn into anger. When the parents got out of sight, we would find handfuls of rocks and throw them at those fortunate brats. I would do anything to earn the love of parents who would stand by me! Never had I met my parents, but I knew that they would be as kind and loving as the ones I stealthily watched from the other side of the soccer field. They surely had to be kind and loving if they were mine.

Lady-Mother

At last, after so many cycles of hopes and frustrations—hopes of having kind and loving parents and frustrations of realizing their absence—it was my turn to be visited by unforeseen fortune. It was a chilly afternoon in November. A late autumn wind blew through my little fingers as I was playing a trumpet in the courtyard of the orphanage during the lunch break. A glitzy black Pobeda[2] entered the courtyard and pulled up at one corner. A chauffeur in a dapper uniform stepped out of the car and opened the back door, from which emerged an attractive lady in her early thirties. She was wearing shiny black shoes and a neatly tailored black coat with fur trim around the neck. I was mesmerized by the appearance of such an unusually elegant person in our orphanage. Not until then had I seen a grown-up woman with such an air of supreme refinement. As I glanced at her with unconcealed wonderment, our eyes met and she noticed my innocent admiration. The lady stood on the playground and started to examine children closely. Her profile looked simple but cold as she cast a long, shadowy glance at the children, most of whom were oblivious of her insistent gaze.

When I returned to the classroom for the second half of the school day, faintly trembling from wonderment, I noticed that this unusual lady was conversing with my teacher. When everyone was seated, my teacher asked me and a girl named O, who was a year younger than I, to step out in front of the class. So we did, standing in silence in front of the entire class of fifty. I felt lightheaded while this lady in the fur-trimmed coat scrutinized us from the back row with the discerning eyes of a chicken sexer. What did this mean? I could not tell for sure, but something of great significance was unfolding right in front of my eyes. As I realized that I was being examined, my heart beat faster and faster. Soon the teacher told us to go back to our seats, and no more extraordinary things happened in that strange afternoon.

A few days later, the teacher told O and me that our mother had come to visit us.

Mother?

Our mother?

Sharp pain and joy pierced my heart at once.

When I followed my teacher to her office, the same elegant lady who had scrutinized us in class was there waiting for us. The teacher told O and me that we were sister and brother, and that the lady was actually our mother, who had finally found us. Then the teacher asked us to wash ourselves and put on new clothes "Mother" had brought for us. Everything was happening so suddenly; the teacher expected us to pack and be ready to leave with the lady. I was just nine years old, and still believed deep down in my heart that Kim Hye-hwa, the nanny who breast-fed me, might be my real mother. Could all this be truly happening to me? When O and I were about to leave the building with the lady, Kim Hye-hwa started to cry and told me that she was glad I had finally found my real mother and asked me to be a good child to her. She was faintly smiling through tears, holding my hands so tightly that I almost wanted to pull them back. The director of the orphanage gathered all the children in the courtyard and announced that if they kept studying diligently, someday their real parents would show up as well. Oh, how many times had I been summoned to those gatherings and witnessed with indescribable envy and pain how other children were picked up by their parents. After each occasion I would run to the stream flowing by the orphanage to cry and pour out my sorrow. But now, it was my turn to stand in front of those envious faces. And my mother was not just any mother! Mother looked like a person from a different universe who rode in a shiny black sedan . . . simple wonderment! I got into the backseat of the nice-smelling Russian-made car, still mesmerized by the quick succession of events that day, and only then realized that I was about to leave the place I'd called home all my life. As the car drove out of the orphanage, I saw numerous faces overlapping one another like a montage—the tear-soaked face of my sweet nanny, Kim Hye-hwa; the stern faces of disciplinarians; and the gloomy faces of my dear accomplices who had pulled their strength together to knock out the stupid Goliath.

As the magical journey to a new home continued, the lady-mother turned around from the front seat to face me and my newly discovered sister O, who also must have been lost in confusion.

"I was really sad to have lost you both during the war. I looked all over the country to find you, and now that I have you both in my arms, I want to lavish you with everything you want. Toys, clothes, sweets, whatever it is, you just have to tell me what you want."

While I was listening to her in a dreamlike state, the black sedan pulled up to an old Russian-style two-story house. Later I learned that the house was located in the exclusive Namsan district by Mansu Hill (*Mansudae*) in Pyongyang, where only privileged people could live. When the car pulled over, a stout man with a huge belly, just like the vice-premier the orphans once persecuted, came out of the house to greet us, telling us that we were no longer orphans and didn't need to struggle any longer under his care. This strange yet pleasant man was our "father," according to our "mother." O and I were simply amazed. Then he led us into the house through the heavy entrance door, carrying one of our small bags in each hand. We passed the dark foyer and followed him to the wooden staircase. Father took us to our rooms on the second floor. My room had a desk, a closet, and neatly folded blankets at the corner—all exclusively for me! I'd never really had anything that I could call "mine" at the orphanage, where everything was shared by everyone. To call these things mine seemed like a miracle, and that strong sense of wonder marked the new chapter of my childhood.

Children of Namsan

It turned out that my father was a high-ranking official in the Korean Workers' Party, the ruling party in North Korea. He commuted to work in a new Russian-made Volga sedan, a distinctive marker of his high status. My mother was the manager of the Eastern Pyongyang Department Store, where one could find practically anything. For its size and wealth of available products, it was nicknamed the "one hundred meter[3] store": its grand façade indeed stretched for a hundred meters, from one street corner to the next. Many times I saw my mother bringing bundles of cash home and putting them in a large safe, which was already packed. I had no idea where they came from, but sometimes I would see money stacked up in backpacks in the closet, from which I would take a bundle if I needed it for any personal expenses.

There was no shortage of anything in the new household. Plenty of everything. Plenty of food, plenty of toys, plenty of clothes, and plenty of well-to-do guests poured in. All the guests brought something for us children—sweets, pocket money, and other things—while they asked our parents for favors: to recommend their sons and daughters for a promotion in the party, to hire their relatives at the department store, to secure certain goods from the department store for them, et cetera, et cetera. It looked as if I had everything I needed for a perfect childhood—a large, comfortable house, busy but influential parents, and the prestige of belonging to the powerful circle of children whose families ran the country. A particularly happy memory from this time period is associated with my first pet. Back then in the 1960s, it was extremely rare for North Korean urbanites to own a family pet, as it was only in the late 1980s that some well-to-do North Koreans started keeping pets. I happened to be lucky enough to rescue a monkey from the city zoo during a terrible flood. All civilians, including schoolchildren, were drafted to clean up the mess left by the flood and my class was dispatched to work at the zoo. I saw a tiny baby monkey at the top of the metal cage trying to stay away from the wet ground. All the other animals had already been evacuated, and I did not know how this one remained behind, but I took him home with me and reared him with care and love. The monkey became a friendly follower of mine. He came to sleep with me every night and often cleaned my ears with his tiny agile fingers. I was so fond of this monkey that I sometimes took him on a bus ride. He would usually sit quietly on my shoulder, busily rolling his eyes and turning his head, observing people sitting nearby. One time there was a child sitting next to me eating cookies. The monkey sat still and studied the child for a while, and then quickly snatched the cookie from the child's hand. Next moment, the bus resounded with the child's shriek and cry. The little monkey was a fun creature but also a troublemaker, and it started to bother me when it came to clean my ears while I was sound asleep. So upon my parents' recommendation, sadly but necessarily, I returned him to the zoo after few months of building intimate friendship.

O and I got along well. I truly believed that she was my younger sister, so I protected her from mischievous boys in our neighborhood. She sometimes came home crying after being harassed by the boys. Every time it happened, I made sure that those little tormentors of my sister got their share of bitter tears. The children in my neighborhood all had prominent parents—vice-premiers and revolutionary fighters—and were shielded from the slightest misfortune. The group of kids I knew then included Go Sin-ja, the sister of Go Yeong-hee, who later became the third wife of Kim Jong-il. Go Sin-ja was older and looked out for me as if I were her younger brother. Most children in Namsan district had a sense of entitlement and arrogance, but many were merely overprotected brats who had no clue about real life. Some of them, barely out of childhood, were sexually curious, watching pornographic films their parents secured from Japan and carelessly left within their children's reach. Some of these kids were even sexually active, which was surprising given the astringent, asexual culture of the North Korean society. When their parents were away, these children would get together in well-protected private residences to drink, smoke, and have sexual adventures. Even if they were caught, nobody could punish them because of their prominent parents. Children of Namsan would sometimes fight against groups of not-so-privileged children from the south side of the Daedong River in bloody hooligan matches. These fights would involve literally about a thousand kids who carried clubs in the back of their pants. There were so many participants that we had to line up in regiments as if we were getting ready for a military battle. Young as we were, we learned organizational skills from a construction project of a TV tower under way in the Mansu Hill area of Pyongyang. Schoolkids—rich or poor, privileged or not—were all drafted to participate. We were organized into groups and rotated, from which we learned how to manage people and work in groups. This experience turned out to be particularly useful in group fights when collaboration and communication were key to victory. When these fights broke out, the district police came to arrest those involved, but the officers were not really after the tireless troublemakers of the privileged Namsan district. They knew all too well who would come to rescue us in case we were arrested, so there was not much they could do but issue mild admonishment.

The children's world in our privileged district was a miniature of the adults' world. It did not take long to learn the hierarchy by observing how other children behaved. Although I was outrageous, I nevertheless did not challenge kids whose fathers held higher posts than mine. By the same token, kids whose fathers were subordinate to mine knew better than to mess around with me. But when occasionally the hierarchy among the children was upset and conflict erupted, it always had some sort of repercussions among the parents. When an entire family was accused as antirevolutionaries, they were stigmatized by the community. If there were children in the household, my friends and I made sure to give them good beatings. The persecuted family would soon disappear from the neighborhood, never to return. One day, the family of one of my close friends, Cheol, was rounded up as antirevolutionaries and sent to the penal labor camp. But ten-year-old Cheol was playing at another friend's house when the arrest took place. Next day, he was captured by the police and sent to the camp to join his family. But even before that, Cheol's ordeal had already begun in Pyongyang, as neighborhood children beat him and broke his arms, accusing him of being the son of a filthy antirevolutionary. Even though I did not participate, I had no sympathy, thinking that the beating served him well. I had no doubt that his family members were poisonous elements in our Democratic People's Republic and deserved to be punished. All the children who witnessed such events never had second thoughts about the crimes of the arrested families.

As the children of the Namsan district entered high school, most of them had to deal with the pressure of preparing for a college entrance exam. Having prominent parents ensured them a good future, but they still had to get into prestigious universities, which required a lot of preparation time. Although a troublemaker and prankster, I wanted to succeed and please my parents. During this time I attended the Mansudae Children's Palace (*Mansudae sonyeon gungjeon*), where I immersed myself in mastering all kinds of sports. What a wonderful place that was! I was particularly talented in judo. The Children's Palace ran a program to recruit and train gifted youth who showed promise in music, dance, and athletics. Children who attended had to have a proven good class background—in other words, they had to be descendants of revolutionary soldiers, peasants, and workers. Go Yeong-hee, Kim Jong-il's third wife, also studied at the Children's Palace then and went on to become a dancer in the Pibada[4] Music Theater Troupe. Three qualities were constantly emphasized to, and required of, the children there—knowledge, virtue, and strength. I was not an academic type, so as far as knowledge was concerned, I was never an advanced student. As for virtue, I was too young to understand the true meaning of it. But then, the society in which I lived defined virtue as loyalty to the Great Leader, which made me a virtuous child. As for strength, physical ability was my genuine forte. I was neither tall nor strong, but everyone feared me for my unflinching spirit. I knocked out numerous opponents, sometimes legally in the wrestling arena and at other times illegally on the streets. Most of them were much larger than I. Life at the orphanage had taught me important skills of survival—when to challenge opponents and how to please supporters—at an early age, and compared to the mostly sheltered children who attended the Children's Palace, I was a different sort, fearless, street-smart, and impudent. Kids in our neighborhood feared and revered me at the same time. I was afraid of nothing, and the whole world seemed to be coming together to prepare for my undoubted success.

Disclosure

"You should care more for the children even if they did not come out of your own belly. Lately you seem too distant and cold toward them."

One night, as I was walking upstairs to my room, I overheard my father's voice coming from behind the closed doors of the master bedroom downstairs. My heart instantly froze. On behalf of O and me, Father was reprimanding Mother. I vividly remember that Mother was in the prime of her life, beaming with health and beauty. Just a month earlier, all the family members had been excited to find out about her pregnancy, and I had just started my second year of junior high school. It had been four years since Mother had found us and brought us home, where I grew to be a carefree and confident child who cherished life and the prospects of a bright future. That sense of a perfect world now silently collapsed. My legs were frozen and uncontrollable tears started to pour down my face. A strong sense of betrayal overwhelmed me. Till that moment, I honestly thought she was my real mother. The day she appeared in that elegant black Pobeda at the orphanage vividly unfolded in my mind. How could it be? Why did she lie?

Some years later, I came to understand why I ended up with these parents for some years. My adopters were merely following the instructions of the Great Leader. Kim Il-sung had just told party leaders to adopt war orphans and raise them as their own children. My adoptive parents were young members of the party who had bright futures ahead of them, so they couldn't afford to ruin their chances of success by not paying attention to Kim Il-sung's instruction. After scrutinizing orphans, they picked a girl and a boy for themselves and cared for them according to the leader's wishes.

Until Mother found out about her own baby, she took good care of O and me. I was genuinely happy, and despite my occasional hooliganism, I was a compliant child. But everything changed. After the disclosure of the truth, I was not the same kid. It did not take long for my parents to notice the troubles I was going through, and they must have guessed the reason. But we never openly brought up the issue in conversation. I simply avoided talking to them. The sense of perfect happiness was irreversibly damaged. After school was over I stopped returning home to attend extracurricular classes at the Children's Palace and often ended up sleeping in parks and at friends' houses. The district police woke me up in the park once and took me home. That night, I had a conversation with Father. He asked me if I would be interested in attending the Revolutionary School (*Hyeokmyeong hakwon*), where promising students were educated in a military-style setting to become the elite leaders of North

Korea. It was painfully obvious to both my parents and me that it would be in everyone's best interest if I left the house. After that, I never saw my adoptive parents again.

I am not certain if O had figured out what was going on when I decided to leave, but she remained with the family afterward, until she got married and started her own family. The day I packed and left for the Revolutionary School, my heart ached as much as it had when I was in the orphanage envying the children with their parents at a track meet.

I was again on my own.

As the car took me to the tall gates of the Revolutionary School, I was burning with a strong desire to find out about my real parents. Who were they? Were they alive or dead? How did I end up in that particular orphanage? Here I was again, all alone in the world with questions that could not be answered.

Revolutionary School

The Revolutionary School was a special institute where teenagers of good class background were given education and training in a military setting. In retrospect, it was an awesome place for a confused kid like me who had plenty of positive energy but did not know how to direct or cultivate it. It was a place for youth who showed signs of leadership. All the students had immaculate backgrounds according to North Korean standards—they were the children of revolutionary partisans or anti-Japanese guerrilla groups under Japanese colonial rule. I was an orphan, and at the same time, my adoptive father had a good background, so I was a natural candidate for admission. We all wore military uniforms and lived together in units like military platoons while other middle school students wore regular clothes and lived with their own families. My gloom at having discovered the truth about my adoption was dispelled somewhat when a brand-new military uniform was handed to me. Those shining buttons neatly sewn along the scarlet red trim of my jacket! The slight smell of benzene when the perfectly folded outfit was entrusted to my eagerly waiting arms! The thrill of putting the handsome cap on my shaven head! The excitement increased when the officer explained to us that the difference between our uniform and the regular military uniform was minimal; ours was distinguishable by a small letter "student" inscribed on the shiny buttons.

In the mornings we studied and in the afternoons we worked on military drills. The North Korean state was invested in grooming future military strategists. The majority of my classmates at the Revolutionary School ended up taking important posts in the North Korean Army. We were often treated to expeditions or excursions. Every child in North Korea has to participate in a pilgrimage commemorating the footsteps of our Great Leader Kim Il-sung. We were told that when the Great Leader was 12 years old, he crossed the Aprok River and walked 1,000 *li*[5] to attain learning. When he reached 14 years old, he again walked 1,000 *li* from Mangyeongdae[6] to Samjiyeon[7] to unify his homeland. These were remarkable achievements for a boy of his age, but our Great Leader showed unusual determination and perseverance from early in his life, which we all must emulate—as the teachers would say. Children participated in the walking pilgrimage every year—the same distance our leader had covered in his journey at our age. We would post revolutionary maxims of the Great Leader on the knapsack of the student walking in front, so that we could walk and learn at the same time. Not all children in the rural areas could participate. They had to be selected and endorsed by their school to join a march to Pyongyang. It was a great festival for all, even though by the end of the march, our feet were raw and our toenails bruised. But if our Great Leader had done it, so must we—so must all of us if we were to carry out his great legacy and fulfill his wish to unify Korea.

Just like at the orphanage, the students were instructed to respect the Great Leader Kim Il-sung as our father. We started every day by cleaning his portrait—we would take it off the wall and dust it outside, even in midwinter when our hands were freezing. Whenever snow fell, we were taken to Kim Il-sung's statues and swept the snow off the ground and stairs so that visitors could keep worshiping the Great Leader. In mild weather, we even wiped the stone ground near the statue with moistened cloths. Military-style education suited my taste because it put much emphasis on hierarchy and discipline. I did not at all miss the home I'd left. Sometimes my adoptive parents called my teachers to inquire how I was doing, but I did not have any desire to see them or talk to them. By the end of my second year in junior high school, I was already transforming into a little man. Just like in the military, students were grouped into regiments commanded by student leaders. Each new student had a senior mentor who would act as an adopted sibling to help them adjust and guide them through their stay in Revolutionary School. My mentor

was a student named Z, who must have been around seventeen when she took me under her wing. She kindly took good care of me as if she were my real sister. She would change collars on my shirts, and whenever there were fights among students, she would always be on my side. One time Z bravely yanked at one of the older boys who pestered me. But for being my guardian protector, she got beaten by that boy. How dare the bully hurt the person who was so precious to me! Outraged by the incident, I made a resolution to become stronger so that nobody could beat my mentor again. I was a real tough guy inside, but I was a puny teenaged boy at first glance. Judging from my unimpressive looks, other boys thought they could pick on me. I detested their assumption and began to lift weights and practice judo every day, to the point that everyone, including big boys, started to pay respect and leave me alone. With close friends, I even bathed in ice water in winter to strengthen myself. Once I earned a decent place in the hierarchy of boys at the Revolutionary School, I started to enjoy a sense of vindication. Self-assured, I even won a silver medal in a nationwide judo competition for youth. I had a good time at the Revolutionary School until I reached the age to either go to college or find myself a vocation. Since I was an orphan raised by the gracious kindness of the state, my future seemed promising. Like it or not, to have that kind of good class background was what mattered the most in North Korea.

2 Living for the Great Leader

To the Sea!

My first impressions of the vast sea in Cheongjin still make my heart churn with wild sensations. Its deep blue horizon and salty breeze enraptures me with raw excitement and portentous delight.

"To all the youth of this country, to the sea, the nation calls you forth!"

The slogan filled my heart with dizzy thrill and resounded throughout North Korea at the time I finished Revolutionary School in the late 1960s. Our Great Leader Kim Il-sung was encouraging young people to volunteer to go to the seaside in order to expand usable land and construct new ports to boost trade and the local economy. This massive port construction was rough work that everyone wanted to avoid, but without a second thought, I volunteered to join the league of youth from the Revolutionary School eager to relieve our Great Leader's concern. At that time I did not consider going to college too seriously, so joining the army to serve the Great Leader seemed an alluring idea. Little did I know that nature could be a rough and cruel beast; I believed that there was nothing that men could not accomplish if they were to follow the guidance of the Great Leader.

We were young, fearless, and unconditionally loyal. There were nineteen of us from the Revolutionary School traveling together from

Pyongyang to the port city of Cheongjin. It was a thrilling journey on a night train I still remember so well. All night long, we sang military songs we'd learned at the Revolutionary School and chatted about our future in the unknown place until our voices started to crack. We talked about how we would irrigate the virgin soil and make our Great Leader proud of our achievement. We also talked about the mysterious future comrades who would greet us in a strange city. It would be my first time living on my own, away from the watchful eyes of schoolteachers, surrounded by a group of loyal friends. How much better can it get for an eighteen-year-old boy?

We arrived at Cheongjin just before dawn. The night air was chilly but refreshing, stimulating our strong desire to live. As I stepped out of the train, I immediately sensed that I was opening a brand-new chapter in life. We all felt famished after the endless conversation and started to look for a place to eat. Not a trace of light was to be found nearby. But soon, not far from the train station, we saw a light flickering in the darkness, which looked like the kind of twenty-four-hour restaurant we were accustomed to. In Pyongyang it wasn't unusual to find eateries serving decent food around the clock, and we spoiled Pyongyangites thought those twenty-four-hour places existed everywhere in North Korea.

"Forward, forward, forward!"

"Break through the enemy lines!"

We goofed as if we were still practicing military drills and dashed toward the flickering light. As hungry as we were, we all howled like famished wolves, dreaming of stuffing our empty bellies. But alas, the illusion of nocturnal light came not from a restaurant but from the rigs on the ship floating on the ocean. Even though with its size and population, Cheongjin deserved the legitimate title of a city—North Korea's third largest urban area—it was not even close to Pyongyang in its living standards. Hearing the gurgling sound of our stomachs, we collapsed by the harbor and laughed. We laughed and we sat there the rest of the night. We had to deceive hunger with more talk until we finally could have our first breakfast in the strange port town at daybreak.

Local people in Cheongjin greeted us with kindness and respect. Compared to Pyongyangites I knew, they were plain, stoic, and taciturn. They had heard that we were from the prestigious Pyongyang Revolutionary School, and nobody dared to mess around with us. Out of nineteen graduates dispatched to Cheongjin, eight of us were put in the same room and formed an inseparable group. We spent practically every day together and did everything together. Everyone seemed to be in agreement that the graduates of the Revolutionary School were untouchable, which naturally put us on a pedestal. Except for one roommate who was given an internship at an automobile factory, the rest were given positions as intern engineers at the construction site to observe and learn how to construct ports and use excavators and floating cranes. Our job was to get up early in the morning, clean and fuel machines, observe how the engineers handled them, and once the daily work was over, to clean and prepare the machines for the next day. Sometimes we would spot octopi stuck in the machines. They were fresh from the sea, large and succulent looking. We would crowd over those marvelous sea creatures and wonder whether we could catch them for a special dinner. The kind of work we provided was by no means coveted by the average person, but everything we were supposed to master amused us. After all, we were so young, just liberated from the regimented environment of military school, and feeling completely happy about the new chapter in our lives. In retrospect, we would have felt the same if the work had been as tedious as wiping the floor or polishing cars, because it was enthusiasm, not the kind of work we did, that made us happy. We were fully embracing the new circumstances and imbibing the youth of our existence. I fell in love with the machines that saved us from backbreaking labor. There was nothing more attractive than technology and construction. What could be a greater way to flaunt budding masculinity than handling such machines? Life in the port of Cheongjin was quickly turning a quirky teenager into a man.

The most exciting event in Cheongjin is associated with a man named X, who was a rare guru of a variety of martial arts—taekwondo, karate, judo, you name it. Formerly he had been in a special squad sent to South Korea on a special mission. All of his comrades were killed, but he miraculously survived and came back to the north. X always carried that incredibly painful aura of a survivor and martyr, which impressed us greatly. Moreover, there were other stories that made us respect him even more. When X returned to the north as the lone survivor, instead of being given a hero's welcome, he was suspected of being a double agent and demoted to a provincial post. On his way to a newly assigned workplace in exile on a train, a conductor started picking on him for a fight. X was already in a terrible state of mind, so he vented his anger and frustration at the conductor by beating him nearly to death. For his violent crime, X was sent to a penal labor camp (*gyo-hwa-so*); when he'd served his sentence, he was released into the harsh environment of Cheongjin. It was our sheer luck that he agreed to become our trainer in martial arts. The eight of us were exhausted as we trained our still supple bodies under X's astringent guidance. He made us run for miles with sandbags attached to both legs and swing bats at a hefty sack filled with rocks. As we grew stronger day by day, nobody in the city dared to bother us. Cheongjin back then was crowded with 3,000 new employees from all over the country. The construction of the new port was under way, and the construction of a railroad and other infrastructure followed. All kinds of riffraff flocked to the city, which needed a large workforce. Kim Il-sung gave orders for each workplace in North Korea to draft a certain number of workers to be sent, and the managers took it as a golden opportunity to get rid of their worst people. With few exceptions, these newly arrived workers were neither intelligent nor strong, and my friends and I made sure that we gave the county bumpkins a good beating with our iron fists and legs tempered by master coach X. For the two years we stayed there, from 1968 to 1970, not a single day passed without a spectacular fight with other workers—small or big, fast or slow, compliant or rebellious . . . it did not matter. We simply had to fight somebody as part of the everyday routine. We even lost our appetite when we skipped fighting. In hindsight, we were nothing but typical incarnations of juvenile cockiness, but at that time we felt we were up to something magnificent, which made us the happiest kids on the entire planet.

Sporting for the Military and Kim Chaek Technological Institute

As 1970 arrived, the North Korean military started to organize its own sports teams. Head coaches toured the country, recruiting gifted athletes. One day, my former judo coach from the Revolutionary School showed up in Cheongjin. He claimed to have spent six months looking for me and wanted to recruit me for his military judo team. The coach pleaded that I join the team, which would fulfill my official military obligation. Like every North Korean man, I had to serve in the army anyway, so I gladly accepted his offer. However, it was difficult to let go of the ideal community I'd found in Cheongjin. My dear friends and the martial arts master were my precious family members, and we pledged that we should stay like brothers till death parted us. As I sat on a train waving at my friends, who stood on the platform watching me depart, my heart ached with sorrow while tears welled up in my eyes. "So long, dear comrades"—I wasn't murmuring "Good-bye" then, but instead, "See you again." Those dear comrades, my fellow travelers whose faces still warm my heart, where are they today? We live under the same sky, but there is no way of knowing. As long as I live, I shall never forsake the hope of meeting them again someday.

Thus I returned to where I came from, my dear Pyongyang, the city of our Great Leader's glory. The heart of revolution, the red capital of our socialist fatherland! I began my military service with aplomb, in the special guard sector where my main priority was to compete on the judo team. The most memorable thing that happened to me in the military took place in 1972, when I was drafted to join the final stage of the construction of the presidential residence that North Koreans call Mansu Hill Memorial Palace (*Mansudae ginyeom gungjeon*). An effort to build underground bunkers was under way when I joined the project. By then the monumental building had been under construction for almost ten years on a site where a large orchard used to stand; from this location one could have a good panoramic view of the entire city, and especially Heungbu Pavilion (*Heungbugak*) across the Daedong River, a special quarter where foreign dignitaries, such as Sihanouk of Cambodia, stayed on state visits. The ground-level construction of the building commenced in 1970 and was supposed to be completed in 1972 as the sixtieth birthday present for Kim Il-sung. The project gained speed as the birth date approached. At the same time, Kim's gigantic statue was under construction on Mansu Hill, for which labor forces were drafted from all over North Korea. However, since the presidential residence was a sensitive project concerning the security of the Great Leader, only military forces who could pledge absolute confidentiality and loyalty were allowed to participate. The chief of the guard team was supposed to reside in a separate unit outside the palace, but for better security, his quarters were inside instead. The residence, where Kim Il-sung lived until his death in 1994, was supposed to serve the dual purpose of a peacetime residence and a wartime bunker. For this reason, it was not a tall structure. However, behind the palace was a taller building of ten stories that contained a large water tank. I still do not know the exact purpose of this building, but I suppose it supplied water exclusively for the palace. There were also large ventilation pipes, large enough that people could walk through, connecting the basement of the palace to the building behind. I still vividly remember that there was a thick layer of lead on the roof to protect the palace from nuclear attacks. Every wall was waterproof. As I participated in the construction myself, I still remember enough details to draw a floor plan of this building. Incredible human effort had been poured into it, and no expense was spared. Silk blankets wrapped pipelines that were supposed to go underneath Kim Il-sung's living quarters. All kinds of expensive trees, Chinese junipers, laurels, and many others, came from different provinces to be used as construction materials and garden decorations. White cement, ground marble, and limestone were mixed to create the best kind of wall finish for the exterior of the building. Thousands and thousands of workers dangling on ropes tied to the rooftop hammered the exterior walls of the Memorial Palace as they descended to the ground. It was a remarkable sight; they looked like zillions of ants against the blinding white wall finish. As the hammering went on incessantly, the ground marble became exposed and shone in dazzling sunlight. The soldiers worked with neither sleep nor breaks for meals, as if they were on a battlefield. Once concrete was mixed, everyone dismissed the thought of taking a break and went on working until the concrete ran out. The soldiers' loyalty to the Great Leader Kim Il-sung was such that everyone voluntarily worked around the clock. The belief that the collective purpose was higher and greater than individual well-being was strong enough to eclipse any other thoughts. A high-ranking military general named Jeon Mu-seok was in charge. Jeon was a man with natural charisma and remarkable leadership—despite his high status in the army, he would joke with foot soldiers and cheer them up with unexpected surprises. One time, in the thick of midday construction, he brought loads of apples and had everyone take a break for a snack. This made already highly motivated soldiers want to work even harder. We worked so hard that even the commanders were worried and urged us to rest, but voluntary manpower was a formidable thing. Nobody could stop us, and the presidential residence came out so solid that even a nuclear bomb would have had difficulty damaging it. The building stood there, a bright, shimmering white, as testimony to the remarkable love all the construction workers had for the Great Leader. When the heroic construction efforts ended, I was rewarded with the rank of a second lieutenant.

Until 1974 I stayed in the army and led a simple life of training for the military sports team. Then the team was dissolved and the military sent me to Kim Chaek[1] Technological Institute for college education. So I, who'd never taken great interest in books, ended up studying mechanical engineering at one of Pyongyang's most prestigious universities. North Koreans regard Kim Il-sung University and Kim Chaek Technological Institute as the top two schools in the nation. I stayed at the institute until 1980 as a member of the college sports squad, which was established as part of the intercollegiate sports network. Kim Il-sung University had a similar sports team, which was then headed by Kim Pyeong-il, the half brother of Kim Jong-il. Our Kim Chaek Technological Institute team was headed by a very kind man named K who took good care of me. K was himself a graduate of the Revolutionary School, so it did not take long for us to bond. We sports team members were always popular among girls, especially those from the countryside who dreamed of remaining in Pyongyang after graduation by marrying a native Pyongyangite.[2] Although I was far from being tall or handsome, I was constantly sought after by those country girls while I played all kinds of sports—soccer, volleyball, basketball, etc. This was the time when I met the very famous Hong Yeong-hee, the heroine of the celebrated revolutionary film *Flower Girl*. I remember her as not being so pretty, but rather innocent looking, with tiny freckles all over her face. So many girls were after us, and life was easy, like a breeze. In the morning I was supposed to sit in classrooms, and in the afternoon I trained. As usual, I was far from being a successful student. Most morning class time was spent on a rooftop smoking with buddies. Instead of advanced mathematics, the members of the sports team were given junior high school-level arithmetic, so we did not have to worry too much about flunking. This is how I managed to graduate with honors from a top university without busting my head too much. While other students were eating rice mixed with barley in the student cafeteria, we sports team members ate white rice with plenty of meat at a faculty club. I remember that at Kim Chaek Technological Institute there were foreign students from countries such as Cambodia and Tanzania, all of whom were sponsored by the North Korean government. Since education was free for all in North Korea—from tuition to room and board—it created much pressure on government finance. Once a nutritionist published a thesis in which he stated that noodles made of barley root were a good source of energy. Eager to save money on student food, the state experimented with the idea. But the coarse texture of the noodles gave its consumers bleeding during bowel movements and the economical idea, no matter how appealing financially, had to be promptly suspended.

In 1978, K, the graduate of the Revolutionary School who directed the Kim Chaek Technological Institute sports team, became a big shot. He was promoted to colonel and was made the director of a political bureau within the Korean Workers' Party. Upon my graduation in 1980, he called me to offer a job as chief of the Wonsan military outpost in Gangwon province. With the acceptance of this job I would be promoted to the rank of captain. I thanked him and told him that I would consider the offer. But when I learned that the Korean Workers' Party had already visited Kim Chaek Technological Institute for a background check on me, I knew the choice had already been made. I did not object to remaining under this caring person's mentorship. So I set out to the small town of Wonsan as the chief of the military outpost. Upon my arrival in this remote locale, not too surprisingly, I found out that I only had five subordinates. A captain with five subordinates! What kind of commander is he supposed to be?

An arrogant athlete from the capital city of Pyongyang, I felt like this small place could not handle my energy. The town itself was not much to speak of, inhabited by people who did not know anything beyond the confines of their remote mountainous basin. However, in terms of the North Korean military industry, Wonsan was a rather important site. It then had five major factories—Munsan iron mill, a chemical factory, a car plant, a pipe factory, and a refinery. It supplied a designated amount of products and energy for the North Korean military. Munsan iron mill, for example, had to supply 10 tons of zinc per year. Five subordinates were supervising each factory, but even to my inexperienced eyes, the supply system was not working well. There was too much corruption and ineptitude among workers and managers in these factories. I devised plans to change that in a short period of time, so I urged my subordinates to spot key managers of factories and gather them for a free vacation. I decided to win their hearts first, so I took them to the scenic tourist site of Geumgang Mountain resort on the east coast, where everyone enjoyed bathing in a hot spa. Then I took them for a tour of Pyongyang and even visited K's office in the Central Committee Building of the Korean Workers' Party. K greeted us with typical generosity and even promised the visitors that he would promote them to posts in Pyongyang if they performed well at their workplaces. Every manager's mind was swollen like a balloon with hope by the time the delegation returned to Wonsan. They must have been in wild reverie, wondering if it would really be possible to move to Pyongyang. While their daydream continued, I set out to reorganize their managerial posts so that they would be under one another's surveillance. I transferred the production manager of the iron mill to the car plant, whose manager was transferred to a chemical factory, whose manager, in turn, was transferred to a pipe factory, etc. Then I went around and told the workers in the pipe factory: "Look, the new manager from the chemical factory has tremendous connections with the Workers' Party. If you don't do a good job, it's going to have a big impact." To the workers in the car plant, I said: "The new production manager from the iron mill has an influential cousin in the army. You'd better show him your best." This way, everyone started to watch their performance and everyone else's. I also made good use of my connections with athletes. The manager of the Munsan iron mill sports team had been a member of the Revolutionary School judo team, which automatically established a very trusting relationship between us. This way I exponentially boosted the production quantity. The year I supervised five factories, we yielded 50 tons of zinc instead of the required 10 tons. For the army's annual consumption of 500 kilograms,[3] this was a remarkable surplus, which could bring in much profit when sold abroad. Back then North Korea exported one ton of zinc for $1,500 to Japan.

Pleasantly surprised by my outstanding performance, K wanted to give me a chance to make extra foreign currency with zinc production. Like every other work unit, the National Security Agency (NSA, *Gukga bowuibu*) within the North Korean military had its own foreign currency–earning department. K knew well that I was a trustworthy subordinate. As an unmarried orphan with no family to provide for, I was not as corrupt as others. As a military athlete, I was used to obeying commanders' orders. I must have seemed the perfect candidate to take on the lucrative task of earning foreign currency within the military unit. Soon after I sent him a report of the surplus in zinc production, he announced that I was going to keep supervising five factories in Wonsan. At the same time, I was being transferred to the Pyongyang foreign currency–earning division within the NSA. The division worked under the name West Sea Asahi Company, a joint venture between a pro-North Korean company in Japan and the North Korean army unit. Even though it had the name of a private enterprise, it operated under direct military leadership to earn foreign currency for the North Korean leader's political bureau. Recruited by a powerful superior who completely trusted me, I was on the way to rapid success and promotion. With an outstanding record of performance under my belt, I was returning to Pyongyang the same year I was sent to Wonsan! K also sent me a Nissan jeep to facilitate my business trips between Pyongyang and Wonsan. With permission to travel for business, I gained mobility to go anywhere I wanted, which was an impossible dream for ordinary citizens, who needed permits even for a short trip. The Nissan jeep served as my companion for more than ten years on every major road in North Korea, from the northern Sino-Korean border to the very southern port city of Nampo, as I drove through, and sometimes intersected with, other people's lives in North Korea.

Marriage and Children

Y stepped into my life as a shy young woman, betraying the stern look of her military uniform. When I first saw her on a date our mutual friends set up, she was a petite soldier whose entire experience had been confined to the regimented life in the army. Never had she ventured beyond what was set out as models of revolutionary life by the party. Not until our first encounter had I realized that someone could look so pretty in a military outfit.

I met my future wife Y in Pyongyang after my job transfer. She had just turned twenty, fresh out of Gang Geon Military School.[4] Y's father was an influential person. He had a Volvo assigned to his post. He had lost his wife when Y was only a child. She was the first of four children, two sisters and two brothers, and she literally became the mother for her younger siblings. My future wife had an appropriate class background, was a party member, and had unflinching loyalty to the Great Leader Kim Il-sung. She worked as a political advisor for the Korean Workers' Party, which was a well-regarded leadership position in North Korea. She was so devoted to the teachings of Kim Il-sung that she sacrificed herself to uphold the Great Leader's ideals: she suffered chronic back pain after she single-handedly attempted to save a large board where Kim Il-sung's instruction was inscribed. "Let us defend Kim Il-sung's great ideals with our own lives" was the phrase she held onto when a gust of wind was knocking it down. She threw herself toward the falling board but was caught underneath it, the heavy board falling on her back. Her love for the Great Leader was such that she was literally ready to defend his ideals with her own life.

We got married soon after our first date. What was there to wait for? She was young, pretty, and had a good class background, and I was longing to have a family of my own. I was twenty-eight and she was twenty. In a typically modest North Korean wedding, we became husband and wife in late 1978. Our Great Leader Kim Il-sung criticized sumptuous weddings as remnants of feudalism and instructed everyone to avoid wasteful ceremonies. He instructed that the ceremony should be as simple as possible and the wedding presents be as practical as possible. There was no such thing as a honeymoon in North Korea. In the countryside, however, the weddings looked much like the ones from the old prerevolutionary days when all villagers were invited to drink and make merry, which often ended in carousing and fistfights. Then villagers would bring cargo trucks and have the newlyweds sit in the front seat while family members and friends sat in the open back of the truck to visit Kim Il-sung's statue and pay respect. Villagers usually had no fancy gifts for the newly married couple, so they would bring things such as a bowl of just-harvested rice or a basket full of vegetables. In urban areas, especially in Pyongyang, things were little different. In the morning, family and close friends gathered in the house of the bride or groom and took pictures in front of a table set up with apples and pears. The newlyweds also bowed to their parents. When this short ceremony was over, two or three cars were mobilized to transport the couple and their family and friends to visit Kim Il-sung's statue in Mansu Hill to lay flowers and pay respect. Then the party moved on to scenic sites in Pyongyang for more photo shoots. We visited Changkwang Street—one of the liveliest streets in Pyongyang—to take our photos. The newly married also exchanged gifts. Normally brides presented their grooms with a wristwatch while the grooms presented their brides with a ring. As I was working at the foreign currency–earning department, I had access to foreign currency stores. So I bought my wife an 18-karat gold ring with some kind of precious stone in the middle, I do not remember exactly what, and also presented her with imported fabric so that she could make a new Korean dress for the wedding day. Normally these ceremonial clothes would not be worn again and simply be put away in a dark corner of one's closet, so families with few resources passed down these wedding garments from generation to generation.

It took Y and me some years to bring our first child into this world, since our first baby was lost on the altar of Kim Il-sung. In every household as in every public space, there is a portrait of Kim hanging high on the wall. Underneath it is a box called a "casket of devotion" where the cleaning supplies—clean cloths and feather duster—are stored. My wife would religiously clean the Great Leader's portrait every morning. That was the first thing she did when she woke up. Even late into pregnancy when she was very close to the delivery date, she kept cleaning, until one day she fell off the chair while dusting the portrait. The shock took our first baby away. After this incident, she kept having miscarriages until we were blessed to see the birth of our first son in 1987.

Children

At last!

My first child was born in 1987 at the Pyongyang Military Hospital. Having grown up as an orphan, I longed for a family of my own. Moreover, since we had lost several babies in succession, the birth of my son B felt like an incredible gift, more than I could ever have asked for. I insisted that my wife deliver the baby at a military hospital, since that was the only facility I could trust for an important occasion like childbirth. Civilian hospitals were short of medical equipment and skilled doctors, which significantly limited their capability to basic matters, such as writing prescriptions, and not much else. Three years later, we were again blessed by the birth of a daughter, J. Although children of the same parents, our son and our daughter were as different as they could possibly be in their nature. If B was a taciturn gentleman, J was a frivolous coquette.

(opposite page) My son is one year old in this picture taken in 1989 in a photo studio in Pyongyang. At the bottom are various studio props featuring the images of happy North Korean youth. The caption at the very bottom reads: "Let us live a hero's life and struggle [for the revolution]!"

(opposite page, bottom) My son and daughter had their picture taken together in Pyongyang on April 15, 1991, roughly two years before my arrest. It is a widespread custom in North Korea to take family photos on April 15—a national holiday celebrating Kim Il-sung's birthday.

1991. 4.15

As soon as she could stand on her feet, I put her on my palms and she would stand still.

It is painful to recall that I was a father who wasn't around too much. Most of the time, I was away on the road on business trips. Naturally I was an extremely poor babysitter. One summer evening when my wife was away and I had to take care of my infant daughter, she cried so much that I wrapped her in a blanket and held her loosely in my arms. She still kept crying, so I kept rocking her. Nevertheless, she started to cry even louder, so I got up from the sofa, walked around, and rocked her even harder. But by the time I got close to the window, I was rocking her so hard that she flew out of the wrap, flew through the window, and fell into a vegetable plot. Thank goodness J was all right, but my wife was outraged to find out about this when she returned and never again entrusted me with babysitting responsibilities.

One thing still breaks my heart as far as the children are concerned: they constantly asked me to give them a ride around for fun, but I could never take them out for a drive due to a regulation directly passed down from Kim Il-sung, who prohibited using public vehicles for private purposes. If someone found out that I was driving my children to school in my vehicle assigned for work, it would serve as a good enough reason to make me lose my job. One time a vice-premier gave his grandson a ride to kindergarten in his work vehicle and was promptly fired to set an example for others. Nobody dared to challenge Kim Il-sung's directions, but the children, simply being children, kept asking for a ride that I was never able to provide.

When my daughter J entered kindergarten, sometimes she brought home candies she wanted to eat at home. These North Korean–made candies were so rough as to make one's tongue bleed. But J savored the goodies and put them in front of Kim Il-sung's and Kim Jong-il's portraits hanging on the wall before she touched any. The rough candies were a great treasure of hers, and she kept them in a secret place. But one day the entire household turned into a pandemonium when she found out that some candies were missing. She immediately accused her brother of stealing. B defiantly denied the charge, but they started fighting like cats and dogs until my wife finally had to yell at J to bring the bag of candies. When she did, my wife noticed that the plastic bag was torn by mice, as she could see obvious teeth marks of the sly little creatures. The missing candies never returned, but at least B could prove his innocence. After this incident, I decided to buy my daughter a large sack of Chinese candies for ten dollars at a foreign currency store. In these stores, privileged people who had access to foreign currency could purchase foreign goods and North Korean souvenirs, such as ceramics and folk crafts. However, North Koreans could not use foreign currency in these stores; instead they used something called "money exchanged from foreign currency," which was like a store coupon with a currency value written on it. Since it was a rule for any North Korean to deposit foreign currency within twenty-four hours of possession, I used the "money exchanged from foreign currency" to pay for the candies. The quality was not much better than the domestic ones, but J was beaming with joy.

"Dear daughter, you should bow to me like you do to our leaders whenever you receive candies," I said, half joking, when I saw her happy face.

Her expression suddenly changed and she told me, looking straight into my eyes without any hesitation, "My teacher taught us we need not bow to our real fathers."

When I heard this, instead of feeling upset, I was impressed by how well educated she was to uphold our great leaders as her true fathers.

Immediately after, she started digging into the wonderful sack of candies, and I was afraid that she might ruin her teeth. So I allowed her to eat only five a day, but one day I discovered that she had had twenty. When I asked her firmly why she'd broken the rule, she bashfully replied: "Daddy, I haven't tried all the flavors yet, and I was getting really curious."

At that point, I simply could not argue with the little eloquent talker.

As I worked in the trading division within the military, oftentimes when the children came back from school, they would deliver messages from their teachers requesting all sorts of favors. Sometimes they would send me letters requesting material support; at other times, they would verbally send their request through my kids.

"Daddy, my teacher asked me today if you could get her some cigarettes," J would tell me when she saw me walking into the house.

"Does your teacher smoke?"

"No, but the kindergarten is working on a construction project, you know. They told me that you would understand."

J was repeating what her teacher told her word for word. Surely the teachers would barter the cigarettes to obtain whatever they needed for the construction project in order to make ends meet.

"How many packs does she need?" I asked.

"I don't know, but we need to give them only a couple of packs each time, because they always ask for more and more."

This time, J was repeating what I'd said to her the last time she'd requested cigarettes on behalf of her teacher. The teachers' requests for material support kept growing as the economic situation in North Korea worsened in the early 1990s. I wanted to do whatever I could, but I soon reached the point when I could not meet their demands anymore. Irritated with good reason, I took time to visit the director of the school and protested.

"Comrade Director, this school must be suffering bad management. How could you possibly request so much from a parent who is mainly concerned about their children? All you seem to care about is what you can get out of their parents, not educating the children properly!" I unleashed my temper and saw the director's lean face grow pale.

"Lieutenant Colonel, I am very sorry to have bothered you. But you might know as well that our school is no longer receiving an annual budget from the government. We have to rely on ourselves to run this place and take care of your children."

The director profusely apologized, but frankly speaking, there was not a single reason for her to do so. As she had said, it would have been impossible to run the school without extracting resources from parents because the government practically stopped providing necessary funding. The frustration I felt was compounded by the somber reality of our deeply troubled economy. The basic needs of everyday life—food, clothing, education—were getting difficult to obtain. There was nothing I could do about it. Nor was there anything the director of the school could do. We could only be resourceful and patiently hope for better.

Loyalty Funds

It would not surprise any North Korean to hear that an economically troubled socialist country is the place where the most excessive forms of capitalism flourish. As far as I can remember, this certainly was true as early as the late 1970s. At that time, as a token of extreme loyalty to the Great Leader, the Chief of the People's Armed Forces, General Oh, submitted a proposal to Kim Il-sung that each military unit set up a department to earn foreign currency to provide for its own expenses, in order to relieve the Great Leader's worries about nationwide economic hardship. Soon after the proposal had been accepted, the Great Leader instructed that each military unit work toward realizing General Oh's excellent plan. Subsequently, the People's Armed Forces (*Inmin muryeokbu*), the National Security Agency,[5] and the Social Safety Agency (*Sahoe anjeonbu*),[6] three mighty organizations in the North Korean military and security listed in the order of their influence and power, each saw the establishment of a foreign currency–earning department within their organization. Each department ran trading companies; the one I worked for in the NSA was called West Sea Asahi Trading Company. In the late 1980s our company's goal was to generate a half million dollar profit annually by exporting lucrative items, such as mushrooms, medicinal herbs, seafood, and the like. However, Kim sent an instruction to raise the goal to a million dollars in the early 1990s and thereby weed out weaker companies, as so many workplaces wanted to run such companies for profit. Our company remained in operation, as it was never a problem to meet the goal of generating the designated million dollars.

As a NSA military officer earning foreign currency for the party, I always had access to various goods and had no difficulty supporting my family. In a semiprivate firm where generating profit was the primary objective, every officer wanted to stand out. The foreign currency–earning department was a small capitalist island in this highly controlled North Korean state—an exceptionally competitive environment within a gigantic system loaded with lethargic and corrupt workers. Competition was rough. Unlike many incompetent compatriots, everyone in the company worked around the clock. In the West Sea Asahi Trading Company, there were around 30 workers, all with the rank of colonel or lieutenant colonel, who were supervised by a one-star general. Although this looks like a very tiny fraction of the entire society, a much larger network of North Korean people would be involved in foreign currency–earning activities. In every province, the West Sea Asahi Trading Company had a branch headed by lieutenant colonels, who would in turn command 300 to 500 local workers and staff members. These local workers would work with other local farmers and workers who comprised the lowest stratum of this state-led capitalist food chain.

Everyone worked so hard, as if they were on the battlefield, in order to generate surplus over the one-million-dollar minimum annual quota.

But since these companies worked under the full protection of the Great Leader and the party and exercised a monopoly over lucrative export items, earning a million dollars was never a challenge. Quite the contrary, each trading company would end up with a surplus, which eventually filled the pockets of the people in leadership positions. If a company worker could contribute to accumulating wealth for his superior, then he would be favored and looked after. This way, a harsh competition among subordinates, akin to the survival of the fittest, was set up to accumulate private wealth for their superiors. Based on my personal experience working for the West Sea Asahi Trading Company, I can say that the total profit was split between the Korean Workers' Party and the trading company on roughly a 7 to 3 ratio, which means that on the average, the annual surplus was well over $400,000. This profit, which did not get absorbed by the party, ended up being used to bribe higher-ups who would facilitate the operation of the trading company, as a kind of investment for future business. Whatever surplus funds were not used as bribes ended up in company heads' Swiss bank accounts or other secret places.

For the West Sea Asahi Trading Company, the main export item was seafood, but exporting mushrooms to Japan was another extremely lucrative business, which was monopolized by Kim Jong-il's office as one of the main resources to earn foreign currency. Our company was brought in to facilitate the operation. Mushrooms of the highest quality could cost as much as $360,000 a ton. However, they had to be exported soon after picking in order to guarantee freshness. This could be challenging. One time there was a group of mushroom farmers who demanded higher food rations from the government in exchange for their crop. In protest, they refused to hand over the mushrooms that were supposed to be shipped to Japan the same day. I knew too well that these farmers were getting only a meager ration for the lucrative produce. They would have fallen unconscious had they known how much foreign currency their crops were bringing in and how absurdly minuscule their portion was in the entire scheme of profit sharing. But since it was my job to make sure the products were delivered to Japan on time, I had to come up with some sort of emergency plan. The company was counting every second to ship the goods, and it would have been counterproductive and even dangerous to directly meet the anger of these farmers. So I offered them an abundant amount of rice wine as a way of opening up discussion, but my plan was to make them drunk. I kept offering drinks while only pretending to drink with them, under the pretense of making peace. The farmers, who were not used to such treats, took advantage of the occasion. When the last farmer was about to pass out, I ordered my subordinates to load the truck with boxes of mushrooms. We had to drive all night to Pyongyang airport without a break to meet the scheduled time for shipment. The final dramatic touch to this emergency plan was to disguise our truck as a funeral car. This was a good idea, as we saved some time at inspection points.

The seafood trade was mostly carried out in the East Sea (Sea of Japan) located between Korea and Japan. When we handed over loads of seafood, I would go on board on Japanese ships to receive cash payment. The Japanese partners, many of whom I befriended, were not supposed to get off the ship. But unless specifically prohibited by the Great Leader, practically everything was possible in North Korea if one had the right connections. So using my network of influences, I snuck my Japanese business partners off the ship and drove them to resort areas where they could hang out with North Korean beauties. These women were well-trained workers who understood that by providing discreet service, they could earn some foreign money for their benefit. I urged the Japanese partners to tip the girls generously and when they left, I checked with the girls to make sure that they were compensated well. Not only Japanese but also my colleagues in the foreign currency–earning department enjoyed having access to these women. Even though we did not seek them out ourselves, there were always offers of women wherever we traveled. We were bound to encounter provincial authorities who gladly paired Pyongyang officials with local beauties. Most of these women knew too well that American dollars and Japanese yen could earn them expensive items hardly available to ordinary people, and they readily provided their sexual services in exchange. Most of them were entry-level party secretaries who were well educated on how to behave themselves and keep silent about the illicit encounter. Many were Koreans who formerly resided in Japan but decided to come to North Korea. These women with overseas experience needed hard currency to obtain foreign goods in order to maintain their previous lifestyle, and many voluntarily offered themselves in order to satisfy their desire to consume.

If these women were high-end prostitutes, at the other end of the North Korean sex industry were streetwalkers who would hang around near foreign currency–only restaurants. They would wait for customers to walk out and ask, "Do you want to buy nocturnal flowers?" When caught, they would be sent to correction facilities where they would be subject to torture and harsh labor, but there was no way of stopping them from earning hard currency the only way they knew how. These women were addicted to expensive foreign clothes or cosmetics and would keep pursuing illegal business even at the risk of severe punishment. The streetwalkers existed well before Kim Jong-il came to power, but as economic hardship affected everyone, the number of women selling nocturnal flowers kept increasing.

My work at the trading company brought me chances to travel to the Soviet Union twice—first in 1982 and later in 1987. The first trip was to Sakhalin, where we discussed the possibilities of future trade with Russia and Japan right on the sea border, which promised to be a more efficient way to trade seafood than to go though existing trade ports. The second trip was to Khabarovsk, where we discussed with Soviet partners the possibilities of expanding joint operation. At that time, both the Soviet Union and North Korea were profiting from the presence of the North Korean woodcutters working in Siberia, who would provide cheap labor to the Soviets and bring back foreign currency to North Korea. One of the things we discussed during the second meeting was establishing a factory to process northern bilberries, which were plentiful in Siberia. Bilberry spirits were very popular in North Korea, but realizing this joint adventure turned out to be more complicated than we initially thought. Each trip lasted for about twelve days, but I saw many things that were different from North Korea. Overall, I felt that the Soviets exercised a greater degree of freedom of speech and spoke badly of our Great Leader Kim Il-sung. They also spoke badly of their leader, Andropov. Although working for the Soviet government, the people we met were rough sailors at heart and became even rowdier when they drank. They spoke freely of everything. They took us visitors to an impressive buffet-style restaurant where an array of seafood was served—marinated herring, smoked salmon, oysters, sturgeon—and everyone could eat as much as they wanted. Small children ran around the table with their rosy cheeks and sharp noses blazed red by the Siberian blizzards. When I gave a fat little blond girl an affectionate pinch on the nose, she smiled back and shrieked: "Nel'zia!"[7]

The fall of 1988 was the most glorious moment of my career as a foreign currency–earning officer at the West Sea Asahi Trading Company. My boss, K, wanted to promote me to a higher post within the NSA by letting me contribute 360,000 U.S. dollars directly to Kim Jong-il under the exalted appellation of "loyalty funds." This was a common practice in North Korea. Many elderly Koreans who were living in Japan and whose children and grandchildren lived in North Korea were avid contributors, as they had access to foreign currency and wanted the North Korean regime to take good care of their descendants. The lavish contributions were not limited to hard currency, but included any goods with considerable value. Once a farmer came across a 300-year-old ginseng root and sent it to the Dear Leader as a loyal tribute. Such events were widely publicized in the media to encourage emulation by others. In 1988 when I contributed my loyalty funds, Kim Jong-il was in need of foreign currency more than ever. That year South Korea was hosting the Seoul Olympic Games, and the world's attention was directed toward the southern part of the Korean peninsula. In order to compete with the Olympic Games, North Korea hosted the grandiose 1989 World Festival of Youth and Students. This festival had been held twelve times previously, but in 1989, its scale became exponentially larger to compete with the Olympics. I still remember how I walked into the Central Committee building of the Korean Workers' Party and handed over my loyalty funds. Within the Central Committee, a director of the 39th Bureau was exclusively in charge of Kim Jong-il's private funds. I spent the following month in happy anticipation, knowing that I would be somehow acknowledged for my contributions by the Dear Leader and the party. Indeed, slightly over a month later, I heard that the Dear Leader had signed a letter ordering the party to look out for my family. In North Korea, such a letter was a guarantor of success not only for myself but also for the entire generation of my children and grandchildren. When such glory was bestowed by the Dear Leader, there were celebrations for the recipient. I was summoned to the Central Committee and received the letter in a solemn ceremony. I was swelled with pride and happiness. My wife was wiping tears of joy. My wide eyed son, too young to understand the meaning of the occasion, was in my wife's arms in wonderment. The next day, the North Korean People's Army newspaper reported the ceremony in a large column, praising my patriotic action in the most flattering manner.

We Are All Happy

As my personal life was evolving along the preset course of happiness—secure job, residency in Pyongyang, marriage, children, promotion, and recognition by the party and the Dear Leader himself—I also saw many unspeakable things that stemmed from systemic problems within the society. In the city of Shinuiju in the early 1990s, there was a group of vagabonds, come from the countryside because the economy there was so bad. People nicknamed them penguins, as they moved in groups and wore dark, tattered rags. They had no place to live or work, so they carried bundles of personal belongings—dirty blankets, dented pots, shoes with holes, and other minor items. They lived mostly by begging or doing odd jobs, such as transporting sacks of imported flour from China and getting a sack as payment. I still vividly see images of those penguins and think that they looked more like refugees from the Korean War era than citizens of the glorious happy socialist republic.

Because my job as a foreign trade official allowed me to travel all around North Korea, I witnessed many tragedies that other people with restricted mobility would not have seen. The situation in Pyongyang was not as terrible as elsewhere, but in the early 1990s, even Pyongyangites were struggling with food problems. The food ration system was becoming dysfunctional just like everywhere else in the country, but the citizens were better off because of power they abused. The ones with influence could usually get whatever food they wanted through underground channels. The ones who had overseas relatives or a chance to travel overseas were also relatively better off than most people stuck in the country because they could get their hands on foreign goods, which were highly desired among wealthy North Koreans ready to pay any sum for them.

I remember how in the early 1980s, I learned about the unfortunate former Korean Japanese (*buksong gyeopo*) in the city of Hamheung. These were ethnic Koreans who had previously resided in Japan but decided to return to the Korean homeland and chose the north over the south as their legitimate land of origin. Because of their ties with relatives in Japan, these former Korean Japanese were known to be better off than average North Koreans. Those in Hamheung were visited by the local party members and were urged to contribute to the construction of Kim Il-sung's statue. The visitors gave false promises of granting Pyongyang residency in return for their donation. Having contributed a handsome amount, one Korean Japanese waited and waited for a reply, became anxious, and started to pester the local party official about the transfer of residency. Annoyed by the frequent contact, the party official agreed to meet the Korean Japanese late at night by a warehouse on the outskirts of town. When the hopeful Korean Japanese showed up, the official chopped off his head with an ax. Then he chopped up the body, put the parts in a trunk, and dumped it into the sea. When the trunk was found by fishermen, the local authorities ordered the murderer to investigate the case! In the end, the criminal was exposed and publicly executed.

There is a less grim incident about a former Korean Japanese that I heard from my colleague at NSA. It was quite common for Korean Japanese to cremate ancestors, put their remains in jars, and keep them in the house. When the time came to commemorate the dead ancestors in an annual ceremony (*jesa*), the Korean Japanese would bring out the jars, bow in front of them, and offer sacrifices. Cremation was not a custom known to North Koreans, so when a pair of thieves broke into a former Korean Japanese's household, they thought that the remains in the fancy jar was some kind of herbal medicine that a rich Korean Japanese had sent to their relatives in North Korea. So the thieves stole the jar, made a potion out of the remains, and guzzled it down like a special treat. When the former Korean Japanese found out about what happened, he was outraged and despaired, but in the end, he had to give up the idea of accusing the thieves, because now they were the only remains he had of his parents and he would have to invite the thieves to sit instead of the jar and offer sacrifices in annual ceremonies for his ancestors!

But not many stories end in laughter.

In the early 1990s at the Chilgol Collective Farm located in Mangyeongdae—Kim Il-sung's birthplace—a horrendous mass murder of thirteen people took place. The incident came to public knowledge when a surgeon went to a marketplace to buy pork for his father's birthday and found unusually fresh meat on the stands. But soon, because of his professional training, he was appalled to realize that what he was looking at was none other than human flesh. He asked the butcher for a price and found out that it was below the market rate. He bought one kilogram and headed straight to the police station, where he threw the meat on the chief's desk and yelled at him.

"You bastards, what have you been doing while an atrocity like this was happening in our town?" the surgeon shouted out.

"What is this crazy fellow doing here throwing meat on the desk?" the chief of police yelled back.

"Look carefully, filthy swine, what you are looking at is human flesh!"

Only then did the police chief realize what he was looking at—that amorphous flesh, still exuding the fresh smell of blood. The ensuing investigation revealed that the entire family of the butcher was involved in the frantic cannibalistic spree, which was motivated by deep economic trouble. The family set up a stand in the farmer's market in town and spotted rather stout peasants who were trying to sell sacks of rice. The wife approached these unsuspecting vendors to buy rice and told them to come to her house to receive payment. When she brought them to her place, located far away from the busy streets, her husband and brother would kill and butcher them with sharpened knives. The men would immediately take out fresh flesh and the wife brought it to the marketplace while the men burned the remaining body parts in a furnace. The team was caught after they had butchered their thirteenth victim. Those in the military in charge of security, including myself, knew about the incident soon after it happened from the criminal report.

Unbelievable incidents of cannibalism are too numerous to list in their entirety, but the common theme among these events is that people will do unthinkable things when they are famished to death. People will turn into animals to survive. In the mining town of Bukchang in southern Pyeongan province, state food rations came to a halt in the late 1980s. Things turned really bad and many disappeared due to starvation by the early '90s. A man in his sixties spent all day looking for grass and tree bark in the mountain foothills, gradually dying of exhaustion and hunger. But one day, he saw a burial ceremony in the mountains as he was leaning against a tree and eating bark. Later that night, he came back to the burial site, dug out the ground, opened the coffin, and dragged the corpse down to his hut. He marinated the dead person's flesh and preserved it in a large jar. When the old man was caught, he was consuming the marinated flesh of the third corpse he had found. Another incident in Haeju in Hwanghae province involves an old woman who went mad and dipped her grandchild head first in a large pot of boiling water. Her daughter-in-law was out to beg for food while the mother-in-law was taking care of the infant. The grandma passed out when she heard the child scream, never to open her eyes again. It was springtime, which was the toughest season for people in the countryside—long before the new crops would yield a harvest and long after the last grain from the previous harvest had run out.

In 1992, I was on the way to Jeongju on a business trip. As I was driving on an unpaved road in the countryside, dry dust rose along the sides.

I saw a woman walking ahead of me, so I slowed down to avoid raising too much dust. As I drove by, I noticed that she was standing there, barely moving. She looked as if she was going to collapse in a minute. I stopped the car and offered her a ride, although this was against the company rule. She was covered in sweat smeared with dust and fatigue. Her reddened eyes were completely covered with mucus. I asked her where she was from and where she was headed. The woman could barely talk due to exhaustion, but after a short break she told her story. Her husband was a worker in a chemical factory in Anju. They had two children, but as the food ration had halted, there was no way to survive in their hometown. So she and her husband each took a child and went in search of food. She was from the farming village of Jeongju, so she left the child at home and was on her way to town, hoping to find some food there. She has eaten nothing for three days and had no idea where the husband and the other child might be. I had some hard-boiled eggs that my wife had packed for me, so I offered her one. She took an egg in her palm but could not lift it to her mouth. Her arms were shaking so hard, as if they could not sustain the weight of an egg. When I dropped her on a small street of her hometown, I looked at her back, walking slowly toward her parents' home. It was a half-demolished hut, and it did not look like the exhausted woman would get much there.

But even before the conspicuous economic hardship began to leave macabre scars in the early 1990s, in April 1982, I witnessed a public execution of a fifty-year-old man in Nampo, a port city near Pyongyang. Back in 1982, the food-rationing program in North Korea was still functioning normally and people had not begun to suffer from starvation. Still, there were many people struck with hardship, especially in the countryside. The executed man worked for a collective farm where he supplied water. One day, when he was working on a plot of land near a mountain, he saw a young woman, a neighbor of his, climbing down the mountain with a large sack on her back. She worked for a shipyard in the same town. One of her supervisors was struggling with neuralgia, and she had heard that azalea brandy can relieve the pain. So she went to the mountains to gather flowers, of which there were plenty on the hills in April. But the man thought she was returning from work with a sack of rice, a food ration from her workplace. When he demanded the sack, the girl meekly replied in shock: "Ajeossi,[8] why would you want this sack?" She was so shocked that she could not continue talking. The desperate man raised a sickle to threaten her, but then he was seen by an elderly man of sixty-five years plowing the land down the hill.

"You bastard, leave her alone, why would you want to kill her?" When the elderly man started yelling at him, the aggressor froze that moment, left the girl behind, and started to chase the man. But ironically, the fifty-year-old could not catch up with the sixty-five-year-old. The latter ran fast for his life and escaped the danger. The fifty-year-old returned to the hill where he had left the young woman. Even though she had had enough time to escape, she could not move an inch because of shock. She was still shivering and in a moment, fell under the swing of the sharp sickle. When the man lifted what he thought was a sack of rice, he was surprised by how light it was, as it was filled with flower petals. Now a murderer, the flustered man returned home, packed all his belongings, and became a fugitive at his sister's, in the next village. There he was arrested, tried, and when the first snow fell in November, brought to an execution ground. I was in Nampo to transport glasses for my superior, K, then and happened to witness this man's execution, where I heard all the details of his crime. In retrospect, 1982 seemed peaceful, but it could have been the very beginning of food crisis that prompted this man to murder a neighbor for what he believed was a sack of rice. The government made a public display of this case to establish law and order, but the majority of witnesses felt a very different sentiment than the one intended. As I remember, the people who gathered at the execution ground saw a dark cloud spreading over the fate of their country where people were destined to kill each other for a sack of rice. Everyone was silent, but their hollow gazes seemed to ask: *What will happen next in the unknown future?* Could we have known back then that this was only a prelude to indescribable tragedy to come?

3 Downfall of a Model Citizen

Family Secret

As my own life evolved into a pattern of normalcy, I became increasingly interested in my own background. Where did I come from? What happened to my birth parents, and how did I end up in the orphanage? None of this was known to me and I burned with curiosity whenever I thought about these questions. But as I was very busy with my work in the trade company, there was little time to contemplate my unknown past. Eventually, my curiosity grew into determination that I should find out about my parents. To have grown up as an orphan gave me an advantageous martyr's status in North Korea, since I had lost my parents while they were defending the country. I also benefited from my adoptive parents' influential roles in the party. Even though we were not tied by blood, having had them as my parents at one time enhanced my profile. But despite all this, I had an increasing desire to find out about the parents I had never met. Every day I was facing the mystery called myself—an enigma that had to be unburdened for me to be able to live on.

I decided to visit my dear nanny, Kim Hye-hwa, the woman who had raised me at the orphanage. I called the orphanage and inquired about her. The year was 1988. She was a retiree living with her stepdaughter in the town of Byeokseong in Hwanghae province. When I had a chance to stop at a business bureau nearby, I visited her house unexpectedly.

"Oh my, my goodness . . . I never dreamed of seeing you today!"

My dear nanny shed a stream of warm tears as she immediately recognized me on her doorstep. I had visited her only few times since moving back to Pyongyang in the late 1970s, and it had been almost ten years since we'd seen each other, but she was the same as before, kind and loving, now simply older and weaker. She was an honorary director of a local orphanage of which her stepdaughter was in charge. I was relieved to see that she was being taken care of by her stepdaughter and son-in-law, who worked for the local party organization. I asked her about how I ended up at the orphanage. Luckily, she had taken copies of all the records of those orphans she personally reared with her when she was transferred from Pyongyang to Byeokseong. She looked up mine and found out that a young man named H had dropped me off. There was a record of his address: Daepyeong village in Hwanghae province. The old nanny copied the address and gave it to me with a significant look.

Soon afterward, I visited the village and asked for H. Villagers told me that the man was now working as the general manager of a food factory in a nearby town. I knew that visiting him might take some time, so I was ready to move on when an old man on the street corner started to scrutinize me and asked, "Isn't your name S?"[1]

I sharply turned toward him.

"Yes, it is," I replied.

"Can't you recognize me?"

The man had ordinary features of an aged person—sagging cheeks and deep dark circles around his eyes, which made it difficult to see them.

"No, I cannot," I murmured.

"Silly me, of course not. You were only an infant when you left. How could you have remembered anything, you poor thing? . . . As for me, I am a very distant relative of your mother."

Having said this most surprising thing, he sighed deeply and lowered his gloomy eyes. A chill ran along my spine. On the one hand, I felt stunned to have met a relation, the first person I knew to be connected to by blood, but on the other hand, I was shocked by the old man's ominous reaction. If he was a distant relative of mine, why did he look so dejected? Wasn't he glad to meet me, if he hadn't seen me since I was an infant? I did not want to ask him anything more. The odd reaction of the old man was like a bucket of ice water poured onto burning curiosity, and I did not feel like inquiring about my past any longer. I wanted to return to my home in Pyongyang as soon as I could, to the familiar faces of my wife and my son, the warm embrace of my loving family.

But on my way back to Pyongyang, a twist of fate made me pass a large sign of the food factory outside the village where H worked. It was just a few minutes away on the road from the village. I could not resist the temptation to put an end to this strange journey of self-discovery. When I drove in, the guards requested my identification since I was not wearing my military uniform but civilian clothes, as I often did on business trips. Upon inspecting my identification they realized that I was a lieutenant colonel in the People's Military and cordially let me in. When I stepped into H's office, he scrutinized me with an arrogant air. He had a noticeably condescending attitude, quite becoming of a general manager at a factory overseeing five to six hundred employees. Under his supervision, they were operating a confectionery, a distillery, and a bakery. During that time of harsh economic conditions, this was a highly coveted position in North Korea. When the state-controlled food ration system could not guarantee distribution any longer, food was better than cash since everyone was willing to barter what they had in order to survive. If one had access to food, it surely meant one had access to power.

"What brings you here?" H asked me, swaggering noticeably.

"I had something to ask you," I answered.

"We do not have any bottles of spirits to give away at this time," he intercepted coldly. Obviously he thought a military officer had come to bully him for free stuff, just like my daughter's kindergarten teachers would ask for free things from me.

"Do you work for a market?" he asked.

"No, I have something to discuss with you," I told him impatiently.

Noticing the seriousness of my expression, he dismissed all the secretaries in the office and closed the door. I waited a few seconds and asked, "Do you happen to know the person by the name of S?"

His face changed that moment. The obvious arrogance disappeared and instead he appeared pale and frozen, dumbfounded by what he had just heard. In unsettling stillness, he glanced over my face; his cheeks twitched, then tears welled up in his eyes and ran down his face in two rivulets.

"I am your maternal uncle. Your mother is nearby, staying in our village," he told me in a trembling voice.

I could not say a single word, nor could I breathe.

After some silence, he continued to reveal my true background.

Uncle told me that I had a sister, a year older than I, who had died of hunger after the Korean War. I had an elder brother too, but my maternal grandmother had urged my uncle to drop me at the orphanage and send my brother to Revolutionary School in fear that we would not be safe with our own family. Uncle was a teenager just about to graduate junior high school when he laid me in a cart and brought me to the orphanage. He left his address, hoping that I would be able to find my way back to him someday.

"What happened to my mother?" I asked, barely breathing.

"I wish you wouldn't ask that question."

"I must know. How in the world can I not ask about her when I just heard that she is alive?"

"We all suffered a great deal because of your father."

My uncle told me that my father worked as a peddler crossing the 38th parallel during the Korean War. Nobody knows what really happened, but the North Korean government soon arrested and executed him for having spied for the U.S. Central Intelligence Agency. My uncle escaped punishment because in legal documents, my parents were recorded as divorced at the time of my father's arrest, and therefore Uncle and Father were no longer related. Uncle later went on to earn his doctorate and became a distinguished specialist in fermentation. Having proved his professional skills and dedication to work, he worried less about being persecuted for having been connected to an American spy.

My brother had come to see my uncle in 1986, two years earlier. But unfortunately, he was not alone. A political advisor from the party came along to verify his class background in order to recommend my brother for membership in the party. My brother was a skilled worker who distinguished himself with diligence and talent, so his superiors had decided to reward him by admitting him. Every North Korean had to have their family background checked and verified in order to be promoted or initiated into the powerful organization. This was why my brother visited his hometown, which he had left at the age of seven. There was simply no way he could have known about the disastrous repercussions his visit would bring. The party member who accompanied him almost fainted when he accessed my brother's file: he did not expect to see the heinous description of "American spy" in the record of a model worker. The party member was a sympathetic man who told my brother he would act as if he'd seen nothing that day. Not having seen his own family record but realizing that there was something seriously wrong with it, my brother urged Uncle to tell him everything. It did not take long for him to realize that he had no future in North Korea. He believed that he'd survived this time, but sooner or later his record would be revealed. It was only a matter of time. To be the son of an American spy is the worst kind of record any North Korean could have, and he seriously contemplated escaping. He gathered a group of friends who shared his plans and prepared to flee. But a hidden spy among the group divulged the plan to the authorities before it came to fruition. My brother was arrested and accused of being the son of American spy who plotted to betray his country. He was shot in front of a large crowd at his own workplace, which had praised him as a model worker. My mother was also arrested upon his execution and was sentenced to hard labor. Having served her term, she had nowhere else to go but her hometown, where she was living quietly, out of sight.

As my uncle was telling the story, my arms and legs became rubbery. There was deadly silence between us. Strangely enough, as shocked as I was, I was thinking clearly at that moment. I was relieved that nobody else was present to hear the story. But had I shown up with a political advisor or a party member who wanted to verify my family background like my brother did, it would have been an irreversible mistake. I would have been arrested on the spot, never to return home. It was my luck that I happened to have visited my uncle informally, but my past had better been kept a secret, even from myself.

"Don't come back. If you can, stay away from here. It's better for everyone because the risk of being seen by others in this town is just too big. Don't worry about your birth record. I will take matters into my hands and resolve the problem so that you will be all set for the future."

Uncle was looking at me with an expression that was both sad and resolute. I could feel that he was ready to make any personal sacrifice to protect me from impending danger.

"But if you really have to see your mother, you can stop by when you are on a business trip and I will arrange something secretly."

I do not remember how I drove back to Pyongyang that night. The smile disappeared from my face and I became increasingly worried. I had a family to look after, and if someone were to find out about my past, what would happen to them? My wife was a loyal party member who had even sacrificed her first child on the altar of Kim Il-sung. How could I reveal my past to her? How would she react? Would she stand by my side? It was tormenting to think about how the person closest to me in the world would respond to the history that I had no control over and that could totally ruin our lives. And my brother? I had a brother! If only I had tried to find out about my future a bit earlier, I could have saved him from making that fatal attempt to escape! But he was lost forever. These thoughts about my closest relatives weighed heavily on my soul, and from the day I learned about my family history, my character changed. I had been a lighthearted, fun-loving jokester, but I became increasingly pensive and irritable, carrying the burden of fatal knowledge—the knowledge that could destroy everything and everyone precious to me.

Fragile Happiness

"Congratulations! Your last name turns out to be Park, not Kim!"

My superior D, who had taken the place of K, was happy to give me the terrific news from my hometown civil registry office. It was 1989. A young dispatch from my hometown was standing by him, obviously satisfied that his message had delighted the high official. "This officer found that your real birth father's last name is Park, so your last name should be Park accordingly. Did you, in your wildest dreams, ever imagine that your full name is Park S, not Kim S?" He looked amused, as he thought that he had unearthed the biggest discovery and could not wait to brag about it. According to the record presented, my "father" was a revolutionary martyr with a perfect class background by North Korean standards. The civil registry said his name was Park Bok-deok, and he worked as a vice-chairman of the People's Committee in Hwanghae province. A perfect professional background! Not only that, Park Bok-deok also died a perfect death, executed by the South Korean security police during the Korean War in 1950. Indeed an immaculate record. It was no wonder my superior was excited, because I needed a thorough background clearance check for future promotions. I too was surprised—not that I had a different birth father, but that such a communist saint turned out to be my father, at least in the record.

As soon as I heard the news, I knew that it was my uncle's work. Soon after my unexpected visit, he must have consulted my mother about how to protect me from impending dangers. Since I had a successful career that led to quick advancement, it was obvious that some high authority would look up my family record for background clearance, a compulsory step preceding any promotion. If anyone had a closer look at my record, my parentage would destroy me. My mother and uncle must have thought it over and come up with a risky idea. She suggested, I learned only much later, that I be recorded as her child with Park Bok-deok, born out of wedlock. Park Bok-deok had lived next door and the two had been good friends. My mother assured Uncle that there would be enough witnesses to testify to their close relationship. Then my uncle summoned an officer in the civil registry department in his district, which also included my hometown, and told him about my case. Uncle explained that unlike other children in the family, I was the son of Park Bok-deok, but because I was born out of wedlock, I had not been registered as his son, which had to be done immediately. This officer, like many others, had been benefiting much from my uncle, who had been giving out spirits, food, and baked goods. He was not in a position to ignore my uncle's plea, so he walked miles to visit my mother to interview her. She persuaded him that I was indeed Park Bok-deok's son. In North Korea, there is a regulation that requires at least seven witnesses when a major amendment in one's civil record is made. My mother supplied eight neighbors as witnesses who all agreed that I looked different from the rest of my siblings and that I resembled the deceased neighbor. Having secured all the necessary evidence, the officer came back to my uncle, all excited, and told him that my birth record would be amended shortly. Soon afterward, he showed up in my boss's office to report that there had been a change in my birth record. Thus far, my promotion cases had been based on the records of my adoptive parents, which guaranteed me a position in the People's Army, but in order to attain a much more exclusive leadership position in organizations that dealt with national security, such as the Social Safety Agency or the National Security Agency, my birth background needed to be clarified in a much more meticulous way.

I decided to reward the messenger who'd brought the news. Even if I did not participate in the making of my uncle's plot, I could quickly figure out that my mother and uncle pressured him to go out of his way to change the record.

"What kind of TV do you have at home?" I asked this quite young-looking officer.

"We have Daedong-gang, sir."

"Black-and-white TV! You certainly could use a better one!"

His face brightened. I sent him not only a brand-new TV but also other appliances, such as a refrigerator, fan, and rice cooker, which were highly coveted items for ordinary North Koreans. I also gave him enough cash for his trip back home. The messenger had an expression on his face as if he had met a good fairy granting all his wishes. I knew exactly what was happening here, but did not say a word out of fear. I also knew perfectly well what I was doing—risking fate, taking a gamble to see how it would go. Sooner or later, someone would have learned my real background, which could have completely ruined me and my family. Fabricating the record was only a preventive measure, but the risk was grave.

Years passed. I carried out my trading business as usual as a lieutenant colonel. But in the back of my mind, I constantly thought about what would happen next. During this time, I asked my uncle to arrange a meeting with my mother. No matter how dangerous it was, I had to meet her. So I visited her twice in my hometown. In a small room in my uncle's house sat an old woman whose face I could not see. I could only see her silhouette moving, her shoulders shaking from suppressed emotions. She cried and cried. To be seated in a dark room with a sobbing stranger who was also my birth mother was a simply bizarre experience. As odd as I felt, there was no emotional rapport. She was a total stranger to me, not having taken any part in my life. I was disturbed by this distance I felt toward her, and after the second brief encounter, I decided not to visit her anymore. All I could do for her then was to help her financially, entrusting my uncle with whatever I could give.

Then in 1993, the NSA made a decision to promote outstanding officers to honor Kim Il-sung's birthday on April 15. To celebrate national leaders' birthdays by promoting model citizens was a tradition in North Korea. I was included in the list of candidates to be promoted to the rank of colonel, so the agency had to do a thorough background clearance of myself and the members of my family. The NSA headquarters looked up my "father" Park Bok-deok's record and called all his family members. It turned out that Park had three sons and a daughter, and I was listed as the fourth son. All of Park's children had remarkable careers in North Korean society, thanks to their communist saint father. The first

A photocopy of a reservist card verifying my status as a military officer in the North Korean army reserve. My name is entered as "Park S," as the card was made after the amendment to my civil records.

(bottom) The cover of a reservist card. The letters read: "Democratic People's Republic of Korea Ministry of People's Force [Ministry of Defense]."

son worked in Pyongyang as a high-ranking party official; the second son worked as a personal interpreter for Kim Il-sung and accompanied him on his state visit to Africa. The sister was married to a brigade commander, and the third son was a political advisor working at the Polytechnical Institute. To the NSA commanders, my promotion must have looked like a perfect occasion for a family celebration—the rank of colonel in the National Security Agency, to which I was to be promoted, was by no means an unimportant post. So they called the first son of Park in Pyongyang and congratulated him on his youngest brother's impending promotion. The first son was puzzled to hear the news and told the NSA headquarters that he only had two brothers and never in his life had he heard my name before. The NSA was taken aback. It had never occurred to my mother or uncle to contact Park Bok-deok's children to notify them of the amendment made to the civil registry, so my supposed siblings were not aware of my existence until they were contacted by the NSA. As for me, I thought that the older siblings would sooner or later find out about the new addition in their family record. I was hoping that they would contact me then, because it was a Korean tradition for the elders to reach out to younger family members. Also, since I was clearly aware of how dangerous it was to falsify any official record, I was afraid of initiating the encounter with my "siblings."

The NSA was run by extremely loyal officers who were at the center of the most sensitive security matters in North Korea. The agency guarded the interest of the North Korean leadership and protected their safety at the cost of their own lives. Only those whose loyalty and class background were 100 percent proven could join. The NSA headquarters was alarmed when it discovered that there was a significant contradiction between my record and the testimony of Park Bok-deok's other family members and immediately ordered the Social Safety Agency to investigate the entire case. The SSA summoned the officer who had personally collected the testimonies of my mother and eight witnesses, cross-examined them, and found out that the suspicion was well deserved. The eight witnesses who had given testimonies about my paternity were simple folks working on a collective farm and were completely intimidated when interrogated by the well-trained agents from one of the nation's top organizations. They simply wanted to avoid trouble and confessed that my mother had urged them to become witnesses in a case they were not sure of. The agents severely interrogated the officer and found out that he had received a handsome cash reward and brand-new electronic appliances when he amended my record. The SSA came to the conclusion that my uncle and mother purposely fabricated the record in order for me to join the heart of Kim Jong-il's most trusted agency. After all, my original family background was tainted in the worst possible ways—two public executions, one of an American spy and the other of a would-be deserter of the homeland. The extreme contrast with the family of Park Bok-doek was suspicious enough for the NSA to assume that I was attempting to infiltrate the most powerful agency in North Korea in order to further the poisonous espionage activities of the enemy state, the United States. No matter what I said, the case was sealed and my future was doomed.

Arrest and Torture

"Tell me how your father passed on his espionage mission to you. What instructions did he give?"

"I have not the slightest idea."

"Tell me how your father passed on his espionage mission to you. What instructions did he give?"

"I have not the slightest idea."

"Tell me how your father passed on his espionage mission to you. What instructions did he give?"

"I have not . . . the . . . slight . . . est . . ."

A bare light bulb was hanging from the ceiling like the face of a phantom. At times, the phantom looked like it had bleak eyes that kept staring at me. At other times the face seemed to have nothing but thin lips that showed a cold, derogatory smile. I was fading away in a dark interrogation room. I was sleep deprived and tormented by a series of events like a prolonged nightmare. The interrogators wouldn't let me sleep for days. But when I occasionally passed into nauseated slumber, I saw the face of the young officer who had traveled all the way to my hometown to collect my record. I saw my uncle's face as his eyes had welled up with tears when I first visited him unexpectedly. And then appeared the faces of my family the day I was arrested. It was an ordinary day—peaceful and quiet. For some reason, my wife hand-washed the Nissan bright and shiny, early that morning. I remember thanking her for it. My son had already gone to school, but my wife and daughter were still at home and saw me off in front of the house. Our white dog was wagging his tail as I drove the car past the alley. That day I drove to the port of Nampo to dispatch an anchovy fishing crew to the sea and supervise the shipping of export items—fresh flatfish and fluke—to Japan, a lucrative business for the North Korean government. As usual, I met my business partners out on the ship, signed a couple of documents of the business transaction, and exchanged the delivery certificate for payment. When I returned to the parking lot by the dock to load my trunk with the briefcases of foreign currency just received from the Japanese business partner, I could not find my car. Instead I saw a group of Social Safety agents looking for me. They presented an arrest order, which bore an endorsement signature of Kim Jong-il himself. My heart froze. Would Kim Jong-il ever have seriously contemplated the connection between the suspected spy and the ambitious young officer who had once presented him with loyalty funds when he signed this order? I have no idea, but I knew that only Kim Jong-il himself could reverse his orders. I immediately knew what was going on. The agents ordered me to get in the backseat of their car, and two of them sat on either side of me. I was silent, but I noticed that at every checkpoint, there were two policemen on motorcycles ready to act if I attempted to escape. This was an espionage case, which required close attention to security. I felt that something I'd feared but unconsciously anticipated had finally happened. The decision to arrest me came from the highest level, and I was a mere victim of the state machinery. But I felt adamant that I personally had done nothing wrong. I tried to assure myself that the National Security Agency would have a better understanding of my case once they knew how, up to this point, I had been living solely for my country, despite my unfortunate family background. The Great Leader would clarify my case. But then I thought of the young officer who had amended my birth record. Was he safe? Was he also arrested? What about my family? What about my mother and uncle? An incident that had happened a long time ago frightfully entered my thoughts: thirty-two family members of a prominent political wrongdoer were all executed. This recollection drove me crazy, and I was burning with anxiety to know what had happened to my family and the officer. If only I had a weapon, I thought, I would free myself, dash into the facilities where they were detained, and rescue them. Much later I learned that my mother and uncle were promptly arrested and sent to a labor camp (*kwanliso*). I am not exactly sure what happened to my wife and children, but knowing the North Korean practice well, I would be greatly surprised if they weren't also sent to a camp. Later I also learned that the officer who had amended my birth record was sent to a coal mine for forced labor. And immediately after my arrest, the entire National Security Agency had to launch a fifteen-day revolutionary struggle to cleanse their workplace of bad influences I, the American spy, might have left. My immediate superior, D, was demoted to a lower rank.

My eyes saw bursting flashes of light and my ear felt unbearable sensations as the interrogator slapped my face with his large fist.

"Tell me how your father passed on his espionage mission to you. What instructions did he give?"

I had nothing to say. They could not have seriously believed that I'd ever had a chance to see my father and inherit his espionage mission, since I was only an infant when he was executed. But they kept going with the same question.

"Tell me how your father passed on his espionage mission to you. What instructions did he give?"

I no longer had the strength to even open my mouth. The pain in my ear brought tears to my eyes.

"You bastard, you dirty son of a bitch, you fucking son of an American spy, how did you receive your espionage mission from your damned father?"

I was completely sleep deprived and could not react any longer. I had lost track of how many hours or days had passed. But I knew that if I told them what they wanted to hear, there would be no other punishment but a death sentence waiting for me. At moments, the sleep deprivation became so severe that I simply wanted to surrender, but I bit my lips to remain silent. As time went by, the interrogator became more and more infuriated by my stubbornness.

I soon learned that I was being held at Maram detention facility, which was located in the Yongseong district of Pyongyang. For the first three days, they treated me well. They put me in solitary confinement. Although it was small, it was clean and had wooden floors. Decent meals with boiled eggs were served. At the same time, they wanted me to write a confession letter explaining my activities as a spy, how I'd inherited my father's defamed profession. They also requested that I clarify my mission at the National Security Agency and confess how I managed to get away with such a huge, deceptive plot for so long. I wrote the letter about my life exactly the way I knew it and explained that I never had any intentions other than serving the Great Leader and the Dear Leader.

I was kept at the detention center for three and half months. During that period I lost about thirty pounds due to daily torture. When I refused to write a letter confessing my treasonous crimes, they started to deprive me of sleep. When that did not work, they stuck sharp bamboo pieces under my fingernails until the nails fell off. The pain was sharp and nerve wracking. When that method did not work, they increased the level of pain and shock. They handcuffed me and hung me by the wrists for hours until the flesh around the wrists was torn. I still carry the scars from that torture to this day. One of the worst tortures I endured was to have my body, waist down, submerged in water in a tiny cell that prohibited me from moving. The cell was so tiny that I had to bend slightly in order to fit my body in. They kept me in that excruciating position for forty-eight hours. When I couldn't stand it any longer and collapsed, they came and dragged me out. When I was not being tortured, they put me in solitary confinement in a tiny cell about two feet wide and five feet long and ordered me not to move an inch. When I couldn't bear the pain any longer, they brought me blank paper and made me write confessions.

Physical torture at Maram detention facility was unbearable, but what was more tormenting was the feeling of betrayal. I had been completely loyal to Kim Il-sung and Kim Jong-il since I'd learned how to walk and talk. It was obvious that everything I did leading up to my arrest was for the greater good of our country. I worked harder than anyone else I knew, presented business plans that turned out to be more lucrative than others', ran organizations more efficiently than conventional bureaucrats, and worshiped Kim Il-sung and Kim Jong-il as feverishly as those revolutionary heroes in movies. It was incomprehensible to me that I would be suspected of this treasonous crime. The great purpose that had defined my life was gone. Guilt by association was injustice itself, and the feeling of betrayal became the worst possible torture that broke me into a thousand pieces.

I could hear numerous voices of other detainees suffering from physical torture, solitary confinement, and nervous breakdown, but I never had a chance to talk to them. The guards were watching us all the time. At some moments when I was not being tortured, I thought of committing suicide, but there was simply no way. Guards were watching detainees everywhere around the clock, so there was hardly any moment of privacy. At other times, I still kept wondering how the party could suspect me of treason; even if my biological parents were criminals, I had grown up in the state-run orphanage under the care of our Great Leader, been adopted by highly regarded party members, and served the country all my life. At still other times, when I was suffering in delirium during torture, I saw the floating images of public executions I'd either witnessed or heard about. The macabre final moments had a powerful effect on all witnesses, as the condemned person gasped for his final breath in this world. At that time, I certainly believed that the executed deserved their punishments and our homeland would be a better place without them. Could I have been wrong? Now that the possibility of my own execution loomed large, I started to wonder if there were others like me on death row who couldn't make any sense of what was happening to them. Sitting on the hard cement floor of my cell, I heard jailors talk among themselves about the various reasons the prisoners had ended up at the Maram detention center. I soon learned that most of them were held on charges of espionage. In retrospect, it was the time when Kim Jong-il was launching a massive revolutionary struggle to consolidate his position as the rightful heir to his father, Kim Il-sung. The campaign aimed at creating fear and subsequent obedience among the people who doubted Kim Jong-il's leadership. The regime probably saw my case as serving their purpose—to create terror and disperse any challenges to Kim Jong-il's rise. Whether I really was a spy or not would not have mattered that much. But all I could see then was the single fact that the charges brought against me were unjust, and I still hoped for clemency once I had a chance to explain myself to the authorities. I completely underestimated the regime's emphasis on blood lines and family background, according to which I was only an imposter trying to disguise my true identity and pass as the loyal guard of Kim Jong-il. But I wanted to yell out to them that I had been living a flawless life marked by selfless dedication, and that I deserved a chance to prove it to my beloved country.

Hell on Earth

As time went by at the detention center, I came to believe that I would certainly be shot to death. This conviction increased as the vice-director of the center came to my cell on a regular basis and yelled at me:

"You filthy son of a bitch, you bastard from a cursed line of American spies. Whether you tell us or not, it's clear to everyone that you've betrayed us. So you'd better tell us the whole story to end this stupid game of silence."

I was on the verge of giving up hope that I would be released alive from the center when the door of my cell opened in the middle of the night.

"Come out, you filthy animal."

The vice-director was standing in front of me with a guard on each side. Having been confined in a tiny cell for what seemed like eternity, I could not stand on my feet. Two guards dragged me to a courtyard where a Soviet-made minitruck was parked. They put chains around my wrists and ankles and dragged me into the back of the truck, of which all four sides were covered. Two armed guards sat next to me. They made me lower my head to the floor and I could not see a thing. I was the only detainee riding in the back of the truck. The engine started and the truck moved. I had traveled all over North Korea on business trips, so I could have figured out where the car was headed had I been able to see out the window. But it was completely dark. I felt that we were moving northeast, but I wasn't quite sure. I thought that they were dragging me to the execution ground, where I would disappear without a trace under their gunfire. As I saw this scene evolve in my mind, my heart dropped: my death would be not only my personal end but also an end to the Kim family line. I was the only surviving child of my parents and I did not know what would happen to my son. As the moment of death neared, anger began to overcome fear. I felt like an idiot for having given my life for the Great Leader everyone was brainwashed to believe was a living god. I painfully regretted that I had neglected my family while working so hard for the Great Leader. I was even ready to sacrifice my life for him at any moment, without hesitation. But what for? It meant nothing in the face of injustice. I was hoping that there would be divine intervention to correct this gross mistake, but the Great Leader himself was the one who'd inflicted this great injustice on his most loyal subject. Why this ordeal when I had done everything I could for him? Why?

I thought of my chatterbox daughter who always nagged, wanting to get various things out of me. Where was she now? Was she able to chatter in her merry little voice like she used to? Then my thoughts drifted toward my son, and the image of his pensive face came vividly back to me. He was a taciturn boy, but thoroughly mature inside. He always thought of his parents' well-being before he thought of himself. As the quiet profile of this little man captured my heart, warm tears streamed out of my eyes and quenched furious anger. My throat swelled from the most intense love and regret.

My beloved child.

My life.

The car drove for two or three hours—first along the well-paved asphalt road of the city, then along bumpy unpaved roads. When it finally pulled over, the guards dragged me out. It felt like about 4:00 a.m.; dawn was still a couple of hours away. Not having been outdoors for more than three months, I felt dizzy. My legs shook. The guards ordered me to kneel down on the ground. At first I wasn't sure where I was, but soon I could see gloomy barracks under searchlights hanging from the barbed-wired walls around the large yard. I was in the reception area of a penal labor camp, not far from the main gate, now tightly locked. There was nobody else but some guards and officers. They dragged me into a nearby compound and removed the chains from my hands and feet. Trying to figure out where I was, I started looking around. As soon as one of the officers noticed my eyes were searching, he shouted: "Damned motherfucker, how dare you gaze around like an idiot? Get on your knees and put your head on the ground!"

Terrified, I immediately followed the command. Then a couple of guards joined him in kicking my head with rough military boots. I almost lost consciousness: the emotional toll that had weighed like death itself during the truck ride nearly drove me mad. And even before I could recover from the shock of surviving what I had thought would be my execution, I was being kicked in the head. The front of my jacket was soaked in warm blood running from my nose. With my head hanging, still kneeling on the ground, I heard the vice-director of the detention center talking to the officer at the reception area:

"The son of a bitch is an American spy. He needs to be completely reformed in your facility."

I realized that the three and a half months of interrogation at the Maram detention center had concluded in a sentence mandating lifetime forced labor. That was not something I had anticipated, and I did not know what to make of it. I'd been certain that I would be executed that day. After the vice-director and the guards from the detention center left, the new guards threw me into a cell where I sat for a while. Without saying anything, one guard stuck in a plate on which leftover food, possibly from the guards' meal, was thrown. Although my lips and mouth were bleeding from the kicking, I ate all of it. That turned out to be the best meal I ever had at that camp.

At 8:00 a.m. a medical doctor came in to inspect me. Then I was taken to a warehouse where I was stripped of my civilian clothes and given a prisoner's uniform and underwear. They were made of coarse gray nylon material and smelled as if someone's corpse had rotted away in them. After I put those on, I was put in a car that drove me up the mountain. On the way, I could see mine shafts everywhere. When the car stopped by another office area on the mountainside, I was asked my name and age and was given a two-hour orientation about how to behave myself. I was told that the prisoners could not talk to each other about anything except work-related issues; prisoners should lower their heads and hold their hands behind their backs when the guards passed by; prisoners should write self-criticisms on their former lives; prisoners should not hesitate to report to the authorities when they discovered other prisoners expressing dissatisfaction; prisoners should not climb the surrounding mountains without permission, or it would be regarded as an attempt to escape and shots would be fired promptly. Then a guard took me to a shaft and handed me over to the mining team. Even in my confused state of mind, I was utterly shocked to face the prisoners there—literally thin layers of dry skin glued to skeleton. Only their wide eyes were glittering on dark faces covered with soot as they tried not to look directly into the guard's eyes. At the shocking sight of these half-human half-ghosts, my heart dropped. The guard shouted to them: "Here is your new team member, show him his work." The head of the team told me that my job was to push the cart loaded with stone. Without any further instructions or explanations, I was immediately put to labor, just hours after my arrival at the camp. Thus my life began in hell, from which death was the only escape.

After two round-trips with the loaded cart, my entire body shook. All my life I was always healthy and on the sturdy side, but during the three and half months of confinement and continued torture, my physical strength had noticeably declined. When lunchtime arrived, I felt like collapsing on the ground because of hunger pangs. The leftover food I'd eaten upon arriving at the camp had long been digested. The lunch consisted of watery soup and a handful of boiled corn kernels and wheat. It was rough and tasteless. Other prisoners were voraciously eating it with rough salt they'd received in the morning. Later I learned that the salt was supposed to serve as the only means to brush our teeth. This is how my first day at the camp began. It was very clear that this was the first step in a prolonged passage to death.

4 In the Mouth of Death

Camp No. 14

In North Korea, everyone knows that a labor camp is a place where life is suspended. One does not live there, one slowly dies there. I was simply another dead soul in Camp No. 14.

At 5:00 a.m. everyone was awakened. By 6:00 a.m. the prisoners had finished their meager breakfast and marched toward the workplace. Since the mine shafts were hidden in deep valleys, nobody could see the sunlight. At 7:00 we were already busy at work. Between 12:30 and 1:00 p.m., we had a quick lunch underground in the mine shaft. In order to go to the toilet, the prisoners had to wait to form groups because there was little light and they had to share one bulb to move around. One person had to carry the lamp and lead the way. Then we came out of the shaft around 11:30 p.m. and ate supper outside in darkness. According to the rules, the work was supposed to end by 8:00 p.m., or by 9:00 p.m. at the latest. However, no guard bothered to enforce this. The only real rules in Camp No. 14 were the guards' decisions. After work, we marched back to our barracks and stayed up another hour for political struggle consisting of mutual and self-criticism. At 1:00 a.m., three hours later than the camp regulations, everyone went to sleep. Before my arrest, I used to sleep eight hours a night, on the average. At the camp, that was cut in half.

Even by notoriously subhuman North Korean camp standards, No. 14 was the worst of them all. To my knowledge, no human being had escaped it alive. Prisoners were beyond the point of feeling hungry, so they felt constantly delirious. But what was really killing us was psychological and emotional torture. No family members were allowed to stay together. Upon arrival at the camp, husbands and wives were separated. Children were allowed to stay with their mother until they turned twelve; then they were segregated according to sex and kept in separate barracks. Once families were separated, there was no way of knowing whether other members were dead or alive. The only chance they might have to see each other was during the public executions when all prisoners were gathered in the courtyard. Other prisoners told me that the conditions in Camp No. 14 were so ghastly that in 1990, about three years before my arrival, the inmates had rebelled, killing half a dozen guards. In retaliation, jailors crammed 1,500 prisoners into an empty mine shaft and massacred them with multiple explosives. After this, the guards became even more iron-fisted, but at the same time, public executions decreased in number, replaced by secret murders. When the guards came and took away some prisoners, experienced ones knew that it might be the last time they saw those fellows. Often they did not return, and that meant that they were no longer in this hell with us.

Sixty people slept in our room, which was about 10 by 6 yards and was lit by only a couple of light bulbs. There was no furniture in the room. Even if there had been books, I doubt anyone would have had the strength to read them. When the prisoners returned from work, they simply wished they were dead. At 1:00 a.m., the guards would count the prisoners and lock them in. I can still vividly hear the squeaky sound of the rusty lock behind the closed doors. When that metallic scratching signaled the end of the day, my heart bled as if the metal lock had penetrated straight into my body. As soon as the guards closed the door, the prisoners fell to the ground and immediately went to sleep. Since there were way too many people crammed into one room, one had to lie down as fast as possible in order to secure floor space. Everyone breathed heavily, as their lungs were filled with coal dust and ash. We slept on the cement floor without any bedding, but since we were in a mining camp, there was enough coal to burn all year round, so heating was not a big problem even in midwinter. However, in the summertime, the cool cement floor was unbearably hard on the back. Prisoners were supposed to stand guard in turns and the transfer of duty to a new vigil took place every hour. It was really impossible to have a minute of privacy in Camp No. 14. In the room there was an indoor toilet made of a large metal bucket. For the first three months, I slept right next to that toilet, as did every newcomer according to the rules among prisoners. It was never completely dark after the doors were locked, as the light bulbs shone dimly. However, there were times when some prisoners slightly missed the mark and splashed shit on my hair and face.

The outdoor toilet was made of hopsacks filled with sand and piled up on top of each other. The prisoners squatted on top of the piled-up sacks. There was no such thing as toilet paper. Everyone knew how to wipe themselves with a little stick. Some privileged people who worked in the kitchens or the pigsty had the luxury of using corn silk or leaves they had collected as toilet paper. Since the mining prisoners lacked exposure to the sun necessary for their bodies to make vitamins, their skin was always dripping pus. There was no mirror in No. 14, so there was no way of seeing one's own physical decline, but by looking at the ghastly faces of other prisoners, I could picture what kind of half-beast half-ghost I had turned into. If there had been mirrors for everyone to see their faces, that horrific sight would have been enough to drive one mad. To add an extra touch to our subhuman appearance, everyone's hair and beard were cropped carelessly by other prisoners when the guards let us use dull scissors once a month. No razor blades were handed out in order to prevent suicide and accidents. Life at Camp No. 14 could hardly be called a human existence. Everyone was serving a lifetime sentence and immediate death seemed like an enormous blessing.

In the beginning I did not speak and tried not to hear anybody else's words or take part in conversation. I had no curiosity about anything. For a month I did not talk to anyone, even though some approached and asked where I'd worked before ending up there. Despite my efforts to stay out of trouble, I almost got raped one night during sleeping hours. Other prisoners, including the vigilant, were in their deadly sleep. Even if they were awake, they did not have the strength to bother trying to interfere. The aggressor had been especially kind to me for a couple of days leading up to the attempted assault. He used an honorific form when talking to me and followed me everywhere I went. From the very beginning, I could sense that he was a snitcher. My experience at the National Security Agency told me so, as did my experience at the orphanage. Having

A satellite photo of Camps 14 and 18, where Kim Yong was imprisoned from 1993 to 1999.

barely escaped the rape by pushing him away with what little strength I had, the next day I beat him hard in the mine shaft when others were not watching. Even though I was exhausted with daily labor and poor diet, I was relatively fresh and could easily knock out any other prisoners. In response, the guards severely beat me in public for touching their collaborator. As a matter of fact, one prisoner out of three worked for the guards, observing and informing on their fellow inmates. Promises of easier work and scraps of food motivated snitching.

From 1993 to 1999, I worked in mine shafts 2,400 feet below ground. It was so stifling and sultry down there that even in the middle of severe winter, the prisoners wore only underwear, and it was difficult to breathe. Every day, prisoners in my work unit would descend to collect coal along a tiny tunnel. There were no elevators; we went down in a small round metal container used to transport coal. When it was filled, another work unit would lift the container up and empty it into a train car. In the beginning, I was out of sync with the other workers in my unit, who moved like parts of the same machinery. Enfeebled as they were due to perpetual hunger, they found ways to coordinate their movement. I could not understand how they could carry on, eating so little and sleeping

A close-up satellite image of Camp No. 14. It features the National Security Agency headquarters where Kim Yong was brought upon his arrival in 1993. Also featured is an entrance to the coal mine where Kim Yong labored more than 12 hours a day.

so little, but it seemed that everyone who had been around long enough had internalized the slow rhythm of prolonged labor. I certainly wasn't used to that kind of work, and nobody had shown me how to dig a mine or load a container. I was always getting in someone's way, and because of that the trailers would be lined up waiting for my portion of coal to be poured in before they could move out of the shaft. I was constantly beaten for tardiness by the merciless guards. One day in the first month after I arrived, I interrupted others as usual. Immediately a security guard showed up. Like all the other guards, he was accompanied by two soldiers with rifles.

"Fucking traitor, it's you again, you delay everyone's work! A filthy bastard plotting sabotage, huh?" As soon as he was done with verbal abuse, he smacked my head with the butt of a gun and I lost consciousness immediately. When I woke up, the head of our work unit was putting bandages on my head. As punishment, the guards reduced the portion of my meal by half for two days. A normal portion was not even a handful of boiled corn kernels and wheat, which was already so insufficient that prisoners who ate only the rationed food died of hunger. So when it was reduced to half, I could easily count the grains of boiled wheat and corn kernels. The head of our work unit, a kind elderly man, voluntarily shared his portion with me for two days and kept telling me, "Please eat and don't die, you have to eat to survive."

I was simply speechless. Despite his kind words, I spent the next month and a half contemplating how to end this miserable existence. I decided to commit suicide. It had been two and a half months since I had arrived at No. 14. The thought of dying was overwhelming, but I hoped everything would end like a bad dream and finally I wouldn't have to start another day like this, worried about mine collapse and sudden kicks in the head. The following day, all I could think of was how to carry out my plan. Coming up with a way to do it wasn't as easy as making up my mind to commit suicide. But by the end of the day, I had an idea. After work, when the miners ascended to the surface in the metal containers, I carried out my plan. Each container was pulled up by sets of wires that were connected by safety pins. As I reached about 2,000 feet above the mining ground, I pulled out a pin from a wire. I only heard a sharp breeze cutting my ears and then lost consciousness. When I woke up, I was lying in a pool of blood in the stream that flowed at the very bottom of the shaft. The head of our work unit had once again wrapped my head with a piece of cloth. His arms were supporting my head. The kind man was looking down at me with teary eyes.

"It's a miracle that you even opened your eyes. I thought you were surely not with us anymore." Endless tears kept rolling over his bony cheeks and fell onto my face. My vision was blurry.

Even in my delirious state, I felt utter disappointment more than deadly pain. How was I still alive to continue on in this hellish place after falling straight down to 2,000 feet below ground? That plunge should have killed me, but apparently, the speed diminished as the container hit the walls a few times, making circles while it descended. Moreover, the container flipped and I was tossed out into the stream, which minimized the injury. When I woke up, I regretted that I could not find a better way to really put an end to this indescribable torment.

There was simply no way of escaping Camp No. 14. It was located in a valley surrounded by high mountains. At rare times when prisoners had a chance to see the sky in the daytime, they saw hundreds of crows circling over the valley. They would flock together and cry out, "kaw, kaw." In Korean tradition, crows are not auspicious birds but ominous symbols. But the prisoners liked the crows' cry, since it sounded like "*ga, ga,*" which means "go, go" in Korean. It seemed as if these birds pitied us for being in captivity and wanted us to be free. I still feel the same sensation of despair when I hear the crows cry.

> Dear crows, flying high and free,
> Do not pity us slaving away to death.
> Even though our bodies are in bondage
> Our spirit is still alive.
> Already thirty-five years passed at this camp,
> With time my tears flow like a river.

The prisoners started to sing this song, composed by an anonymous predecessor, when they were brought out to work on a road expansion project. Road construction work was much better than mining because at least we could breathe fresh air. But these types of special projects were rare and didn't last long. While I was working on the road, I encountered two Caucasian prisoners who looked like they were in their late sixties or seventies. They were just like the Korean prisoners—leathery skin and bones. The only difference was that their noses were bigger and their eyes were colored. I saw them from two or three yards away. One of them had a totally bent back. I couldn't figure out why they were there, but they might have been prisoners in the Korean War and have spent a long time in the camp. During the special road expansion project, I also had a chance to see women for the first time since I had been arrested. They were as skinny as chopsticks and had absolutely no breasts. But among the crowd there were some women in better condition. They must have been working at the pigsty and stealing animal feed or working in the kitchen. Or they might have been receiving food scraps from the guards for snitching. There was simply no way for me to know.

As soon as the construction ended, large military trucks started to come in and out of the medical facilities on the other side of the hill using the newly expanded road. The prisoners believed that live prisoners were used for medical experimentation. Crows would flock over the hill and cry, flying in circles over the suspected medical laboratory. All the large military trucks, with hatches covering their backs, came in and out at night. To my eyes trained in foreign trade, it looked like they were carrying freezers in the back. But there was no way for me to verify what the trucks were transporting, or whether live human bodies were really being used for experiments. The prisoners assumed so because there were regular medical checkups, after which the relatively healthy ones were taken away. They never came back. It was also common knowledge that the guards who worked at the medical facility often had retarded children with birth defects. Even the toughest guards avoided Camp No. 14 for reasons like this, and the ones who were sent there were the most merciless.

In addition to enduring backbreaking labor, prisoners were supposed to submit written criticisms of other prisoners four times a week and self-criticisms twice a week. This was done during the daily study session at night, when everyone was in complete delirium, fading away into sleep. At times, criticism would take the form of a public presentation. Only on Sundays were we free from this ritual, due to the rotation of security guards. There was really nothing to confess, but we all had to come up with something in order to avoid severe punishment. Writing self-criticism was hard labor of the mind. Some prisoners used the occasion to receive more food. When they submitted particularly important information about society, the guards offered them a full bowl of corn. Everyone was so hungry, but some weaker ones submitted false self-accusations to get an immediate reprieve from unbearable hunger, even though they knew they would soon be punished for the confessed imaginary wrongdoings. Another psychological punishment was the complete absence of any kind of media—newspapers, TV, radio, there was nothing at Camp No. 14. The separation from the rest of the world was unbearable. On rare occasions when the authorities wanted to reward the prisoners, they played popular songs, such as "Arirang" and "Moranbong," from loudspeakers. That was the most festive thing prisoners were treated to.

There were threats and dangers everywhere, but our worst enemy was hunger. Eating enough to survive was a war in itself, since each meal consisted of watery soup and a handful of boiled corn kernels and wheat. It was impossible to live on that portion, not to mention work twelve to fourteen hours a day in a coal mine. Prisoners died of malnutrition all the time. Miners were so weak that it took them an hour to do the work that would have taken a normal person ten minutes. The hunger was so severe that even rats disappeared almost completely from the camp. The rats were fairly big, and were regarded as a special treat and a source of protein for the lucky ones who caught them. The guards prohibited this, because it was believed that rats were good at predicting mine shaft collapses. One day, I spotted a huge rat while carrying lumber to support the ceiling of the shaft. I knocked it out with a stone and ate it immediately from head to tail, raw, without skinning it. The meat tasted like honey. On another lucky day, I picked up a zucchini on the road near the barracks. A farmer supplying produce for the guards might have dropped it from his cart. I was never fond of zucchini before my imprisonment, but that raw one was so delicious.

One evening I saw that a worker in our unit had found a small snake in the mining area, stoned it, and wanted to eat it. But he was so weak that he could not hold the snake tightly when he put its tail in his mouth. Not quite dead, the snake escaped his hands and bit him, but he was still eating the other end. The other prisoners jumped to grab parts of the snake and gorged on them. The man died two days later. In the camp area there was farmland irrigated by oxen, which were cared for by outside contract laborers. When they passed by the camp on the ox carts, the famished prisoners would go after the animal dung to dig out undigested corn kernels. Anything that moved was eaten—grasshoppers, lice . . . anything and everything in order to survive. On one lucky day a rabbit got lost and came into the shaft. Everyone went crazy. We knocked its head with a stone and ate the whole thing raw. Had the guards known about it, we would have been severely punished. But everyone was insanely hungry all the time. Luckily, since infancy, I had been trained to eat just the allocated portion at the orphanage, and this habit continued well into my military days. So I was more accustomed to enduring hunger between meals than others. Outside the camp, people received special meals on the birthdays of Kim Il-sung and Kim Jong-il, but inside, there was no such thing. The only special treat I remember receiving was the shells left over after beans had been crushed to make oil. They were as hard as a rock and were usually given to farm animals, but when the prisoners received bits, it was an occasion to celebrate. The bean shells themselves were disgusting, but any change from boiled corn and wheat was very welcome. In this place where everyone was half delirious from perpetual hunger, working in the kitchen was a huge privilege. One could at least eat enough corn. Security guards would reserve these highly coveted positions for their snitchers.

The most tragic of all memories related to hunger in the camp is of a man named Myeong-cheol, who was a meek and kindhearted person. We worked in the same team, so I knew him personally. One fall morning we were marching toward a work site, accompanied by the armed guards as usual. No. 14 was located in a deep valley covered with chestnut trees. In the fall, chestnuts were dropping from the trees left and right. The family members of the guards would bring out sacks to stuff them with chestnuts, but when the starved prisoners attempted to collect some, they were immediately shot to death. That day Myeong-cheol could not resist the temptation and stepped out of line to grab a chestnut. It must have taken only a split second, but an accompanying guard saw him and smacked his head with a rifle butt. The weak man immediately fell to the ground.

"Beast of the worst kind, whoever told you to grab a chestnut?" The ruthless voice resounded harshly in everyone's ears. As soon as the guard finished his sentence, he pulled his trigger. The next second, we all saw how the prisoner's head had exploded.

"Throw the bastard away out of sight," the guard indifferently yelled at two other prisoners. Even though everyone was used to sudden deaths, this particular one was shocking for the guard's explosive brutality. The dead man was tightly holding a chestnut as he was dragged to the burial ground, leaving dark scarlet marks of blood as his last trace on earth.

There was another unforgettable incident related to hunger in Camp No. 14, an accident: the shaft collapsed and five prisoners were buried alive. When we dragged them out, they were already dead. We were told to wrap the dead bodies in straw mats and discard them, but two of our team members were so hungry that they cut off a leg from a dead body and hid it in the shaft. They came back to eat the raw flesh the following day. They were discovered by the guards, who immediately shot them to death.

Just like in real society, the camp had a definitely established hierarchy among the population, with the stronger ones coercing and manipulating the weaker ones. Strong prisoners would not usually go out of their way to punish anyone who irritated them. A strong one would order his retinue to pick on the opponent and wait until the opponent joined the fight. Only then did the strong one jump in to restore order and punish his opponent. Usually at that point, security guards would intervene and punish the weaker prisoner for initiating the trouble. As this process was repeated, the weaker opponent learned not to bother the stronger ones. The stronger ones were better fed as well. They received tribute from the prisoners who worked in the kitchen, many of whom had earned their jobs by informing on others. They needed the strong ones to protect them from other resentful prisoners. The guards knew this very well and therefore did not punish the exploitative ones. In fact, the strong prisoners functioned like assistant guards appointed by the real guards, living and working with the prisoners.

But not all the guards were cruel. The elderly ones who had been around a long time were not so strict about the rules. It was the younger ones who were mostly cruel and abusive. They had plenty of energy to wield their iron fists and vent their anger on prisoners. However, I remember one particular man who guarded our work unit, a young chap. Sometimes he would subtly reward prisoners upon whom he wished to bestow favor. When we were working in the mine, he would smoke nearby. Since I had been a chain smoker before entering the camp, the smell of a burning cigarette would painfully bring back the days when I was living a normal life in society. Amid backbreaking labor, I would have reveries about my past, triggered by the guard's cigarette smoke. At such moments, the guard's occasional complaint snapped me out of my daydreams.

"What a bitter cigarette! Terrible taste! Pew! Hey you, come here and clean this!"

He would throw a perfectly fine cigarette on the floor and walk out. The cigarette had just been lit and was still burning. The appointed prisoner would immediately jump on it and puff away the heavenly bud while others intensely watched the orange flame and smelled the air with fathomless envy. Guards were not supposed to stay with one work unit too long so that they wouldn't develop any personal attachment to particular prisoners or possibly the entire unit. If the guards detected any humane connection between their colleagues and prisoners, they would report it to their superiors. And the next day every guard would be rotated to take charge of another work unit.

Mother

One day during work I was summoned by a guard. My heart sank. Was this the end of my dismal existence at last? Other prisoners must have thought that I was doomed like so many others who were summoned, never to return. I got in a container and ascended to the outside of the mine shaft. The brilliant sunlight overwhelmed me. For the two years I'd been at Camp No. 14, I hadn't seen any sunlight except during the brief road construction project. My entire body was itchy and dripping pus for lack of sun. My face must have looked simply awful. As I was facing the sun, tears kept flowing from my eyes. I finally made out a four-wheel-drive vehicle parked in front of the entrance to the mine. The guards ordered me to get in. Riding in the car, for the first time in two years, I had a bird's-eye view of the camp from farther up the valley. The car came down to the main area of the camp and the guards took me to a reception area, quite similar to where I'd been checked in two years before. Many more guards were waiting for me, unfamiliar faces, definitely not the guards from this camp. Out of habit, I kneeled on the floor and lowered my head. One guard who looked like a leader said, "Do you know why you are here?"

I had no answer. I really had no idea. But I knew for sure that I wouldn't be executed; otherwise, they would not have brought me here to the office.

"Read this form and sign it. It's very important for your own security."

The form he gave me said that I could not divulge any information about Camp No. 14 to anyone in any form of writing or speech. The head of the guards threatened in a low, coarse voice that if I opened my mouth, I would be dragged back to the camp and beaten to death like a stray dog. I immediately signed the paper, avoiding eye contact with the guards.

"The Great Party generously considered your case and decided to bestow clemency, so that you could move on from Camp No. 14."

I simply could not believe my ears. My entire body was numb with shock. For a few minutes, I thought that I was excused of my charges and was to be released. I could not believe that I was leaving this hell. I was so carried away that I prostrated in front of Kim Jong-il's portrait and hailed him with what little strength was left in me. "Long live the Dear Leader! Long live the Dear Leader! Long live the Dear Leader!" The guards did not stop me and let me go on until I ran out of breath.

When I was done paying my profuse tribute, the unfamiliar guards ordered me back to the car again. We drove for some time and I saw that we were crossing a bridge over a river. Then to my surprise, I saw a large iron gate. I felt like my head had been struck by a hammer. I knew better than to think that they would let me walk away from Camp No. 14 alive, but I'd been so shocked to hear the announcement that I lost my judgment temporarily and assumed that I was being set free. Of course, that never could have happened. What would happen to me now? The car drove through the iron gates and the guards took me to a reception area, where there were not only local security guards but also guards from the Pyongyang National Security Agency. Having been a part of that organization, I immediately knew that the NSA guards had been dispatched from the capital. There was also an old woman in rags quietly sitting in the corner. She looked completely frozen, as if she wasn't breathing. When I entered the room, one of the guards pushed my back, steering me toward the old woman, and asked, "Hey, aren't you glad to see your mother?"

Mother?

How strange that name sounded in that bizarre moment. I did not know what to say.

All I saw was a crooked face covered with wrinkles and multiple traces of indescribable suffering. Her skin was so thin and dry that it looked like a worn-out rag covering her protruding cheekbones. Her thin gray hair barely covered her tiny head, making it look like a skull with corn silk patches stuck on here and there. The old woman's dull eyes were gazing at me like I was a stranger. She was at a loss. I cannot rationally explain, but instead of feeling glad or surprised to see her again, I just felt incredible resentment toward this strange old hag.

"Stupid cow, don't you realize that it's your son?" one of the guards reprimanded her.

She lifted her head a bit and kept looking at me blankly.

I could see that the guards were looking at each other and exchanging signs. The ones from Pyongyang were also noticing the obvious lack of familiarity between the old woman and me. Later I realized that it was their final test to see if I had really been involved in my mother's conspiracy to forge my identity. Having confirmed what they probably knew already—that I had not had any substantial contact with my mother ever in my life—the officers left the room. The local guards shoved us to the exit and yelled coarsely, "You will be allowed to live with your mother from now on. Now both of you are dismissed." That was how I was suddenly transferred to Camp No. 18 and unexpectedly reunited with my birth mother.

When the guards released us, Mother led me to her quarters. Her gait was heavy and slow. She neither looked at me nor talked to me. She opened the door of a shabby hut made of corn stalks and mud. I could see the exposed stalks where dried mud had fallen out. The hut would collapse if there were a strong storm. The floor was exposed ground, nothing covering it. In a corner of the hut was a small kitchen where a steel pot and a broken bowl were the only household items. This was where Mother had been living ever since she'd been arrested. When we were left to ourselves, we sat in silence. Strangeness lay between us. She kept looking at me from the left, then from the right, and then left, and repeating the process. Her eyes welled up with tears, which rolled down her cheeks in streams. I felt that tyrannical fate was leading me through a tumultuous spiral where I could not see an inch ahead. My head was spinning, and I lay down on the floor and fell asleep without understanding the meaning of it all.

That night, I woke up to find my face covered with tears. When I opened my eyes, Mother was looking down at me. A fresh tear fell on my face. A strange and sore sensation came over me and I gazed into her eyes.

Both of us were speechless, but there was an emotional rapport when our eyes met.

"Mother . . ." I responded to her teary gaze in a low voice.

Mother.

It was the name I'd longed for all my life, the word that I had wanted so badly to pronounce, without any pretense or doubt. There was the mother I'd craved in the days at the orphanage. Then followed an adoptive mother who did not love me. And now in front of me was the mother I had lost, unknown to me, for a reason larger than any of us.

We both could not sleep that night. Mother broke her silence and started to tell me about the past. About the father I had never known, about how Uncle took risks to save my life, how she regretted it after she gave me up at the orphanage, how she wondered about me all her life. We sat and talked; we talked and cried; and when we cried together, we understood each other. Mother told me that my father was a talented mechanic and traveled frequently to Seoul as a peddler. When the Korean War broke out, he became the village chief of the Self-Defense Corps and killed many communists. When the South Korean Army and the allies marched up north, he facilitated their advance. She wasn't sure if he really worked for the CIA, but as far as she knew, it was true that he worked under the command of a U.S. Army officer.

Thus began two and a half years of my life with Mother at No. 18. Being with her made everything bearable. Whenever I had spare time, I would go up the hillside and collect any edible weeds for her, and she in turn would also collect anything edible to feed me. In the beginning I did not know that she was saving a major part of her ration for me. She thought she could get by with less food because she did manual labor, whereas I kept working in a coal mine. Everyone in No. 18, young or old, had to work. My mother's work was to weave plant material for carts and make brooms. Whenever I noticed that she was not eating, she would say that her old body couldn't digest coarse food. Prisoners in No. 18 ate half of what normal people would eat. We had to survive for ten days on a portion that normal people would consume in five days. Our main diet consisted of dried cornmeal boiled with any edible grass we managed to collect. So when Mother cut back on what was already a meager portion, it must have rapidly weakened her. But she was only too glad to put up with perpetual hunger for her only surviving child. For the first time I experienced unconditional maternal love. Her love was strong and pure; it defied any doubts or fears.

Camp No. 18

Compared to No. 14, No. 18 felt like heaven. By 7:00 a.m., all prisoners were required to sign in at their workplace, whereas in Camp No. 14, everyone was at work by 5:30 a.m. At No. 18, prisoners could live with their family in a single hut. No matter how dilapidated the living quarters might

A close-up satellite image of prisoner housing in Camp No. 14. Kim Yong was confined in one of these barracks, approximately 10 yards by 6 yards, with some 60 other male prisoners.

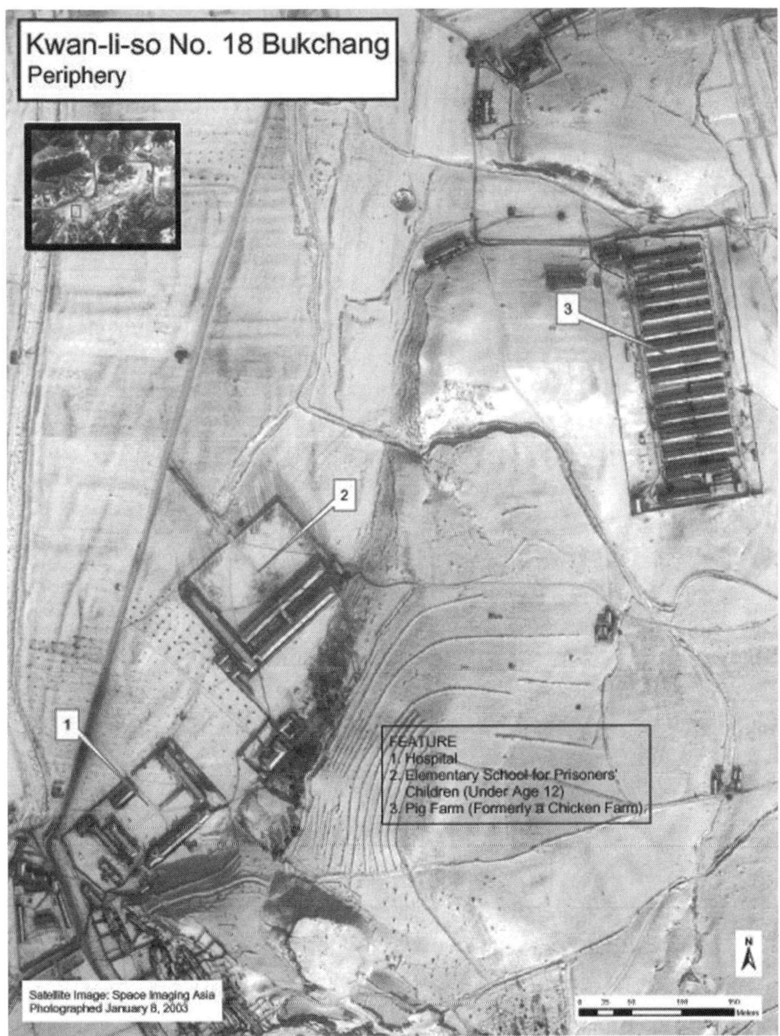

A close-up satellite image of Camp No. 18, featuring an elementary school, a pig farm, and a hospital.

have been, it was humane to live with one's family. No matter how hungry the prisoners might have been, they could at least be with their family members. At Camp No. 14, sixty male prisoners slept together piled on top of one another in a small barrack. There, prisoners were not given any freedom to move around the camp, while in No. 18, they could climb up the mountain to a certain level and gather grass to supplement their diet. The only rule was that they had to return to the camp by a certain hour. For this reason all the bark on the pine trees in that area had been consumed by starving prisoners. If the guards caught inmates collecting bark, they were punished for damaging state property. If the prisoners were caught three times, they would be executed for their intention to destroy state property. Nevertheless, they risked their lives, scrambling to get their hands on anything edible. Although Camp No. 18 was a lot better than No. 14, I still witnessed so much brutality—death by starvation and public executions prevailed.

Only much later did I learn that my former supervisor D had filed for clemency on my behalf, which must have been risky for him. He must have argued that I was sent to the camp not because of the crime I had committed myself, but because of what my parents' generation had done. In other words, I was not the "first generation of wrongdoers," as they would put it in North Korea, but the "second generation" imprisoned for my parents' crime; therefore, D had a chance of appealing for my transfer. Besides, I had been perfectly loyal to Kim Jong-il and his regime before imprisonment. Because Camp No. 18 was less ghastly than No. 14, the second and the third generations of wrongdoers were usually detained there. The original "wrongdoers"—the first generation—and the second generation were often executed immediately upon their arrest; the third generation was sent to No. 18, where the fourth generation was born. In principle, prisoners did not have the right to bear children at the camp. But because family members lived together, women occasionally became pregnant. Many were forced to have an abortion at an early stage. I heard stories about how the guards injected salty water into pregnant women's wombs and dug out the fetuses with spoons. It was not a secret that starved inmates would eat aborted fetuses instead of discarding them after the "surgery." But some women who were discovered too late to have an abortion managed to give birth at the camp to a generation of people who knew no life beyond the walls topped with barbed wire. They were detained there for having been born into a family of "criminals."

However, because they had not committed a crime of their own, they did relatively easy work, such as working in the distillery or feeding the pigs, where they could scavenge food scraps to fight starvation. Guards poured night soil into the animal feed so that the prisoners would not steal it, but this failed to deter them from drinking and eating whatever was in the pigsty. When the pigs gave birth, usually to ten or twelve piglets at a time, the prisoners working there would steal two or three and put them in a boiling food pot. Then they would secretly have a sumptuous feast, unimaginable by any camp standards. They ate not only the tender meat but also everything else—skin, feet, eyeballs, and ears.

In addition to the second, the third, and even the fourth generation of wrongdoers, there were quite a few former grandees in Camp No. 18. Kim Chang-nyeong had held a distinguished post in society when he was a member of the Social Security Agency in charge of selecting agents to be dispatched overseas. Everyone coveted his position of great power, but Kim made a fatal mistake, aligning himself with the wrong people, who fell out of Kim Jong-il's favor. There was another man who used to be a central party officer. He was charged with espionage for personally receiving a Japanese weightlifter, Inoki, at his house when the Japanese visited North Korea. He claimed that he had done this as a sign of hospitality. Those in power knew that the harmless reception of the Japanese was only an excuse covering the real reason for arrest. Just like Kim Chang-nyeong, the officer had sided with people who were not aligned with the Dear Leader Kim Jong-il. Not having done anything wrong personally, and believing that he would explain his case—just like I did when I was arrested—he decided to appeal. He wrote long letters of petition to his friends in Pyongyang but could not find ways to send them. Finally he was able to talk one of the guards into delivering the letters. However, when the messenger brought the mail to the "friends" in the central party office, not all of them regarded themselves as friends of a Japanese spy. Some reported this incident to Kim Jong-il himself, and according to the Dear Leader's directions, anyone involved, no matter how insignificant they might be, was arrested. One sultry day in August 1996, a truck loaded with fifty or so people arrived at the execution ground. Some of them were freshly arrested while others were familiar faces in the camp. Among them was also the guard who had delivered the letters. The camp authorities were really shooting the messenger.

In 1997, Camp No. 18 welcomed a new group of inmates from the town of Songrim. They were former workers from a steel plant producing the best quality steel in North Korea. The town was famous for having received the blessings of the Great Leader himself, who directly reaped the benefits of the plant's products. But in 1997, for constantly starved workers, steel became a means of survival—a product they secretly exchanged for low-quality Chinese flour only suitable to feed animals. The hungry workers could not help but choose food over national pride simply in order to survive. When Kim Jong-il found out about this, he was already battling low morale, and he wanted to make an example out of what North Koreans later called the "Songrim incident." Kim ordered the National Security Agency to dispatch an entire corps to encircle the town. The soldiers ordered the townspeople to stay in their houses and started searching. Twenty-four of the residents had more than three sacks of Chinese flour. They were all dragged to the outskirts of the town and publicly executed, without a trial. The ones who had fewer than three sacks of Chinese flour were rounded up and sent to the camp. Among these were many loyalists who had devoted their lives to serving the Great Leader and the Dear Leader. Their hard work had been distinguished by People's Medals and Laudatory Medals, but facing constant, unbearable hunger, they had to follow their instinct. Their only crime was their need to eat in order to stay alive.

I could not sleep that night. Although my entire body was aching from the day's hard labor, my mind was set on fire. I shook with pain and anger at what I had witnessed that day. Loyalists to the state were rotting in this hellish place where death would be far more desirable. I thought of how utterly deceived the newly arrived from Songrim had been. In fact, everyone in this country was deceived, made to believe the false promise of a better life. And when a person simply wished to survive, they had to pay with their life. That night I lay straight on the floor, clenched my teeth, and felt warm sweat moistening my tight fists as I thought, *I will survive. I have to survive. I will, I will, I will, I will! I will!!! Survive and tell the world about what I have witnessed. Otherwise, this insurmountable tragedy will be forgotten, never known to the rest of the world. I will survive to tell it myself. I will.*

Rebels and Collaborators

There were many children in Camp No. 18, second- or third-generation prisoners who were paying for the crimes their parents or grandparents had supposedly committed. They were in the camp because the North Korean state attributed collective guilt to the families of political wrongdoers. The first generation—the real criminals—had to go into the coal mine and provide the hardest labor. The second and third generation also had to provide hard labor as long as the criminal in the family was alive. Only after the first generation died were the second- and third-generation prisoners treated as lesser criminals by the state. This system sometimes invited unbelievable actions. There was an incident of patricide in Camp No. 18. Three sons, all in their thirties, collaborated and killed their father to free themselves from backbreaking labor in the mine shaft. When the guards discovered the crime, they brought out the sons for a trial. The three sons argued that the person they had murdered was not their father, but an enemy of the state who had frequently betrayed the communist fighters during the Korean War. I saw how the sons proclaimed, with great defiance in public, that they wanted to relieve the worries of the Dear Leader Kim Jong-il by getting rid of the bad element in the state. The camp authorities were pleased with these statements and labeled them as "corrigible" prisoners. I personally witnessed this and two other cases of patricide in Camp No. 18, one of which included a daughter murdering her father for the same reason.

While some children regurgitated the state rhetoric to avoid trouble and lead a slightly more comfortable life, there were also invisible rebels in Camp No. 18. Like all spaces in North Korea, the guards' offices displayed the portraits of Kim Il-sung and Kim Jong-il, which were meticulously dusted and polished. However, at times, the glass covering the portraits would be broken and scattered on the floor. Anyone caught venturing to do this certainly would have paid with his or her life. And there would be days, although very rare, when the electricity at the camp would be cut off and no work could be done in the mines. Some prisoners must have risked their lives to commit this sabotage. Some broke the camp rules just to protest, but many did so simply to survive. In the fall when the corn harvest was imminent, the hungry prisoners could not help going into the fields to steal. Camp guards rotated with fully loaded guns to protect the crops. If they noticed a movement in the field, they immediately fired randomly at the tall corn. Despite the grave danger, the prisoners had to go on stealing; otherwise hunger would kill them. Because I was eating part of my mother's ration, I dealt with the hunger better than others. My mother's sacrifice allowed me to survive.

Single prisoners were grouped together in several barracks, just like in Camp No. 14. They were in poorer health than the prisoners who lived with their families. I worked with many single male prisoners, who often collapsed in the mine shaft. Their bony bodies were then loaded on a two-wheeled cart and sent to the clinic. Doctors at the camp clinic were also political prisoners. Most of them were highly skilled intellectuals and some had even been trained abroad. There were doctors with degrees from Russian and Eastern European academies. But no matter how good they were, the camp did not have any medicine or medical equipment to cure the ill. For this reason, many camp guards preferred to be diagnosed by doctors in camp rather than see their own doctors in society and then secure necessary medicine through connections for their private use.

Camp guards benefited much from their prisoners' former connections in society. One guard who knew that I used to work in a trade department took advantage of me. He would call me over to a private place and ask in a stiff manner:

"Hey, I am going to Pyongyang soon. Do you have anything to say to your friends there?"

"What do you need, sir?" I would reply without looking at him.

"I could use a new color TV," he would reply indifferently.

Then I had to write a letter to my friends in the electronics supply department and ask them to provide a TV set for the guard who bore my note. My friends would recognize my handwriting and signature for sure. When the guard presented the letter to them, they would notice that he was from Camp No. 18 and figure out what was going on immediately. Out of friendship, they probably would have treated the guard well on my behalf and told him to take good care of me before they handed him a brand-new TV set. Then the guard would come back and really take care of me in a surreptitious way. The guards at Camp No. 18 were given dried corn as animal feed for their own household. While the prisoners were starving to death, the guards received food for their stock on a regular basis. When the entrepreneurial guard received his portion of dried corn, he would call me to a warehouse by a pigsty and make me load a bucket full of corn. Then he would make me carry it to my hut while he followed me with a pig. We both knew that other guards were watching us and we had to pretend that we were part of the ordinary scene—a guard directing a prisoner to transport stuff. When we reached the hut, he crassly told me to keep the animal feed there and quickly returned to the pigsty with the pig. When it first happened, I did not know what he really meant, so a few days later, I asked him, "Sir, what should I do with the corn?"

"You do whatever is necessary," he curtly replied, but till the end, he never openly told me to go ahead and eat the corn.

At other times, he would call me to his office and say, "You son of a bitch, clean this tray as quickly as possible."

He pointed to a waste bin crudely made of dry straw. He shared an office with other guards and used the normal language any guard would use to prisoners.

The waste bin contained a few pieces of candy. I quickly sorted them out and put them in my pockets before anyone saw them. When I sucked on a piece of candy, I could feel the difference immediately, the sensation of a small source of energy surging in my body. That's how weak I was then.

But those sweet moments did not last long. The guards were constantly rotated among work units in order to prevent any possibilities of developing human connections with the prisoners. Most guards were strict about rules and went exactly by the book. They had almighty power; if they wished, they could kill any prisoner at any moment. Unlike regular prisons where each inmate's term ended at a certain time, the camp provided no hope for release, and because of that, there was a silent agreement that anything, absolutely anything, was possible. Among the newly arrived inmates were many pretty women. High-ranking officials from Pyongyang, if they were labeled as antirevolutionary, were sent to the camp with their entire family, including their young daughters. These girls had known no hardship before they ended up in the camp. All their lives, they had been pampered with Japanese and French cosmetics and fine clothes, completely unavailable to the general public. The guards took advantage of them upon their arrival and kept them quiet with threats. Then the girls were made to take relatively easy jobs, such as cleaning office buildings and giving traffic signals to trains. It was so conspicuous which girls were sex slaves of the guards. There was a good-looking girl named Jeong-sun who belonged to this group. Before imprisonment, she had been in an all-female music band that was famous for having attractive members and would often entertain Kim Jong-il and his close retinue. It was never made public, but many knew that the group provided "all sorts" of entertainment to North Korea's highest leadership.

Jeong-sun was sent to the camp because she had divulged secrets about the sex lives of some leaders. In Camp No. 18, she continued her job as usual—the entertainment of leadership. She was given the task of checking the attendance in one of the factories. But just like in society, Jeong-sun could not keep her mouth shut about her nightly work. Three days after the rumors spread, she was found dead in the mountains, shot when she "attempted to escape," according to the guards. But in reality, the guards must have asked her to go and gather berries at a certain spot. The executioner, who must have arrived there before unsuspecting Jeong-sun did, easily shot her for attempting to escape.

These kinds of execution were frequent. There were many children who were tempted to go to the riverside to catch fish. Their parents must have warned the little ones to stay away from the river, but young as these children were, their playful minds sometimes forgot about the warning. When the guards found them by the riverside, they fired without the slightest hesitation.

There was a shooting range in Camp No. 18. Trucks sometimes brought loads of people from the outside, but instead of putting them in the barracks, they executed them there. There were many rumors about who these people were, and many were suspected to be the senior officials of the state. It looked like Camp No. 18 was the place to execute the condemned. The regime must have regarded the camp as the black hole of the universe where they could dump their dirtiest secrets. For this reason, the camp guards, no matter how low their rank, wore the uniform of the Social Safety Agency as a reminder that they were obliged to protect the darkest secrets of North Korea. When they returned to society to attend meetings or visit other offices, they changed into regular army uniforms.

Seeing Mother for the Last Time

One day Mother disappeared without a trace. A search began. A day later the guards found her lying unconscious in the mountains. Obviously she went up there to gather edible grass to make soup for me, but since she was chronically starved, she lost consciousness and fainted. In No. 18, the rules mandated that inmates should return from the mountains before 5:00 p.m. If they did not, the guards immediately saw it as an attempted escape. Patrols found her on the hill, and even before interrogating her or charging her with trying to escape, they kicked around the frail woman in her seventies, handcuffed her, and dragged her back to the guards' office. When I returned from the mine at 10:30 p.m., the guards summoned me. As soon as I showed up, they smacked my head with their large hands.

"Son of a bitch, your mom attempted to escape from the camp site. Did you not conspire to escape together?"

"No, sir. She might have been gathering grass to eat. That's all." I felt desperate.

"Don't lie, you damned motherfucker, you must have helped her try to escape!"

Then a couple of them kicked me around with their military boots.

Mother was immediately transferred to special quarters for prisoners condemned to die. The guards kept prisoners there only while they were deciding on the method of execution—hanging or shooting. In the daytime, the detainees would do extremely harsh labor. At night, they were not allowed enough sleep and were forced to do self-criticisms. I was so consumed with worry that a few days after Mother's arrest I decided to secretively go and watch them work. C, another prisoner with whom I was on friendly terms, accompanied me to the site. They were by the riverside, moving huge rocks to build a new pier. Most of the workers looked very young, and Mother looked like a tiny mouse among them. We visited the site around lunchtime, so I happened to catch a glimpse of how the workers lined up for a handful of boiled corn kernels. Since everyone was starved, they were rushing to get their portion, but Mother could barely walk, disturbing others who wanted to get ahead. The guards came to drag her out of line and tied her to a hammock that hung from a wooden stick, which the prisoners used to transport heavy rocks. If my friend hadn't been holding me back tightly, I would have grabbed stones and started throwing them at those bestial guards. In trembling silence, through a stream of tears, I saw how Mother was desperately hanging onto the pole to keep from falling to the ground. Her entire body shook with the futile effort to hang onto life. That was the last image of Mother I saw. Later I heard that she lost the ability to go to the toilet on her own.

About a month after I had seen Mother's last suffering, I escaped Camp No. 18.

A Risky Plot

I had lost my mother forever, but out of that loss was born a burning desire to learn everything about my family. Now I was the only surviving member of my generation and had to understand why such tragedy had befallen us. I simply had to survive to discover the unknown part of our family history. Mother used to encourage me to escape even before her final arrest. She felt she was doomed to end her life in this atrocious place, but she believed that I still had a chance. I wanted to escape in order to fulfill her wish, but had I attempted it, I would have surely caused my mother unbearable suffering. In No. 18 guards chained prisoners whose family members went missing and hung them with their feet barely touching the ground. The chained ones remained in public sight, unable to eat or go to the toilet, until the case was clarified. The humiliating display was meant to teach everyone a lesson about what would happen to family members if one tried to escape. I had witnessed how those hanged faces turned dark in suffering. This was a lesson learned well, and I did not dare to put my mother in that situation by escaping for my own sake. But now that Mother was simply counting her days to die and I had no hope of seeing her again, I became obsessed with how to realize her wishes. It was a risky idea with almost no chance of success.

However, the more impossible it looked, the stronger my desire grew. I was obsessed with clarifying my family history, and that would be possible only if I were alive and free.

The idea of escape had occurred to me when I was transferred to Camp No. 18. The conditions at Camp No. 14 were so severe that I could not even think of the possibility. No. 14 was the worst kind of camp since it imprisoned the enemies of the state. Even the guards there acted as if they were on a war front. However, at Camp No. 18, where the second and the third generations of the enemies were imprisoned, the guards were more humane, and there was more freedom to move around. Knowing Mother's death was certain, I made up my mind and started to study the surrounding areas carefully. There was a river flowing by the foot of the mountain. I thought of diving into it and breathing through a reed, but I was too weak to swim under water for nearly a mile to reach a safe area. So I abandoned the possibility and soon felt lucky not to have chosen that escape route. I learned that the guards cast many nets in the river that would send signals to their office if large objects were caught. The inmates did not know about this until the guards found the body of a former party official who had committed suicide by throwing himself into the river. After this I thought about hiding inside the supply trucks that transported rationed food to the camp. Getting into a truck would be less of a problem than getting out of it. There would be too much risk involved in trying to emerge at the right time, because the doors were locked from the outside and I did not know how to open them from within. I also thought of escaping in a train that transported coal to the outside world, but it obviously would not work: when the loaded trains left the shaft, a large metal press would descend to the open top of each car, loaded with coal, to compact the load and make sure that nobody was hiding inside. No human being could survive that heavy metal pressure. Then I turned my eyes to the mountains, but soon learned that it would be even more difficult to escape that way. There were not only rows of high walls topped with barbed wire but also numerous traps in between the walls that would tear escapees' bodies into pieces. The prisoners learned about this when some were brought out to clean the traps and were delighted to find some rabbits caught down there. They were dead, but still fresh enough to eat.

However, there was one incident where an inmate succeeded in escaping No. 18 by the mountain route. He was a young man imprisoned for supposed treason his father had committed. The young man was a former member of a special force in the army where he received a high level of training and was groomed to carry out very difficult missions. He had already been sent to South Korea twice. His father was a central member of the Korean Workers' Party, but through political conspiracy, the entire family was subject to accusations and inevitable downfall. All four members were sent to Camp No. 18—mother, father, son, and daughter. Like many other new arrivals, the young man's father was dumbfounded that a hard-core loyalist like himself could end up in a political prison camp. He thought it his duty to correct this grave mistake, primarily to spare his family unjustified punishment, so he wrote a hundred letters to party members, pleading his innocence. Then he managed to bribe a guard to send those letters to Pyongyang. The son was also shocked at the misunderstanding and wanted to clear himself of the charges. Unlike his father, he did not write letters to be delivered to Pyongyang but used his well-trained body to carry them himself. At the time he attempted to escape, he was still fresh, not yet crippled by hunger and labor. He managed to steal a rope from the camp and waited till dark. Then he climbed to the top of the hill where the first fence stood. He climbed to the top of the fence, threw the rope to the second fence, and crossed between them without touching the ground studded with deadly traps. After he managed to get out of the camp, he headed straight to Pyongyang. There he went to the central party office building, scattered into the sky the petition letters he had prepared, and declared that he was wrongly charged with conspiracy and that his only aim in life was to serve the Dear Leader with all his might. Then he slit his stomach with a knife as a sign of fidelity to the regime. It was obvious that he escaped because he wanted to protest the charges, just like I had vainly hoped to do when I was arrested. I guess he was hoping that Kim Jong-il would notice his efforts and grant him and his family clemency and exoneration, but whether Kim Jong-il heard of this or not is unknown. The protestor was taken to the hospital to be treated, and when he recovered, they sent him back to the camp. There he was severely tortured for three months. When he was brought out to be publicly executed, every prisoner was surprised to see that the healthy youth they remembered had shrunk to half his former size. He looked like a little stray dog on the execution ground. When prisoners were executed, the other inmates were supposed to witness the process and then line up to throw stones at or spit on the corpse, denouncing the dead. When I approached the dead body, I noticed numerous traces of harsh torture.

Thus I came to the conclusion that using the front gate would be the best idea. Surprisingly, the security there was relatively loose. At 2:00 or 3:00 in the morning, the front entrance was as quiet as the night itself. Maybe the guards did not expect anyone to be so bold as to walk out of there. The gate itself was very tall, but the walls adjacent to it seemed reasonable enough for me to climb. But there were two vicious dogs that would chase me to death if I took that risk. I would have to find a way around them. Securing grilled meat to pacify the dogs was one solution, but how? And even if I got some meat, could I cook it without the other prisoners noticing the smell? Having thought through all my options, I decided that climbing over the front gate when a strong rain shower was pouring down would work. The dogs would not be able to trace my smell as sensitively and people would not hear my footsteps well. I decided to quietly wait for the right time.

Nocturnal Fugitive

Then one day, a totally miraculous chance came unexpectedly.

As I look back, it was more than luck that the chance to escape fell in my lap. There must have been divine guidance leading me to take the risk. That day started off just like any other day at work. Everyone showed up at 7:00 a.m., ate the usual meager portion of boiled corn and wheat with salt, and worked until our backs felt like breaking. But at the end of the day when we were ready to load coal onto the train, the last step in the long daily work routine, we found that there were scattered grains and corn kernels at the bottom of each car. The trains must have just transported food. It wasn't the first time this had happened, and at such rare chances for extra food, no matter how scarce it might be, all the prisoners went crazy trying to gather grains. Despite threats and harsh punishment, nobody could stop them. My work partner and I were also searching every single corner of the train to gather one more grain. That was when we discovered that the floor of the car was unstable. My work partner was a close childhood friend from the affluent Namsan neighborhood in Pyongyang. Like so many others, he had aligned himself with a boss who had fallen out of the Dear Leader's favor and ended up in the camp. On the floor of the car was a thin metal panel, about two by three yards at the largest. There were other prisoners in that car, but even though they saw the metal panel, they were so distracted by the grain that they paid no attention. My friend and I immediately realized that this was something extraordinary. The guards soon appeared and started to whistle and curse at the prisoners. Frightened by the guards and happy with their handfuls of grain mixed with soil and dirt, the prisoners went back to work. But my friend and I could not simply leave behind our amazing discovery. So we remained, risking severe punishment if we were found by the guards. Luckily the car was parked in a dark spot, so unless someone approached closely, it was difficult to see us in the general darkness in the shaft. When we tried to lift the panel, weak as we were, it felt very heavy and we could not do it with bare hands. So we took a lever and moved it inch by inch. We were soaked in sweat by the time we could see what was beneath the panel. There were three holes in the dilapidated wooden floor of the train car. At that time North Korea was experiencing a terrible economic crisis, and the state did not have any funds to maintain property or repair damage. As a temporary solution, they must have thrown in the metal panel to keep the grain and coal inside.

When we saw what was underneath the panel, our eyes met and our hearts froze. We both knew what it meant: a golden opportunity never to be repeated again. The metal panel lay flat on the wooden floor and there was no space in between, but if we stuck a large piece of coal into one of the holes and covered it with the metal, room would be created for just one person to hide. We could climb in and out through one of the two remaining holes in the bottom of the train car. But there was a question still unanswered: Would the metal panel be enough protection from the weight of the metal press and the coal? It was at the very bottom of the train where the press could not reach. *Whether it works or not,* I thought, *I will die anyway if I stay in camp, so I might as well die trying to escape.* Then the idea looked feasible, which made my heart beat faster. My friend's eyes met mine again. We exchanged so many thoughts silently in that split second. Who was going to take this chance? Obviously, there was barely room for one person, and we both wanted to escape. There was not much time to think. It must have been around 11:00 p.m., approximately four and a half hours after we'd entered the shaft for the night's work, which normally lasted from 7:30 p.m. to 1:00 or 2:00 a.m.

The train would start loading soon. Having cleared that particular car, the other prisoners had moved to the rest for their meager harvest. We had to act quickly. We found a largest piece of coal, shoved it into the smallest hole, and pulled the metal panel back on top. That way the larger hole would be reserved for entrance and exit and there would be more space between the metal panel and the wooden floor. At that time, I must have weighed about 88 pounds, whereas my friend weighed more. We both tried to get into the space, but I fit better because of my smaller size.

"Here, you quickly get in and I will pour coal on top." Finally my friend opened his mouth. I knew how difficult it was for him to give up that golden opportunity for me, but I was so glad that I could not concede.

"Thank you, thank you, thank you so much, I will never forget . . ." My throat felt the sensation of something warm and painful and I could not finish my sentence. His eyes were filled with sorrow and he embraced me. His warm tears fell on my face.

"Friend, I hope you succeed, I hope you reach the outside safely."

I could not say anything.

We only had minutes until everyone came back to their posts after grain picking. I quickly got under the car and crawled into that tiny space. It all happened so quickly that I only understood the potential grave consequences of what I had done when I heard the sound of falling coal on top of the panel. What if the guards found out that I had disappeared in the morning? By 10:00 a.m. they would surely notice. At that moment, gruesome images of the publicly hanged prisoners came to my mind. Would people end up throwing stones and spitting on my dead body like we had done to the hanged young former special agent? His tattered shoes were almost touching the wooden platform where the gallows were set up, baring the tortured ankles covered with dark bruises and blood stains. His head was silently hanging, but when I passed by, I felt the eerie sensation that he was still alive, looking down on me. Although his face was bloated like a purple balloon and every tiny blood vessel in his eyes stood out, I felt that this guy had not completely departed. I had never believed that one's hair could stand up at frightening thoughts, but when the image of the hanging body came back to my mind, I felt as if all my body hair stood up. I do not know how much time I thought about the dead ones, but the train started moving. Then my thoughts shifted to the metal press that would descend on the open car by the entrance to the mine. I was not sure if it would kill me or not. Anything was possible, and I literally felt like yelling out loud to stop the train so that I could get out of the car. When I heard the metal press descending onto each car lined up ahead of mine, my body shrank. When the coal in the car where I hid was pressed down, I closed my eyes. The large piece of coal that created the space between the metal panel and the floor cracked slightly and the panel descended a little, pressing my body down even harder. The weight of coal above me restricted my breathing, and I was soaked in cold sweat. I became completely restless, as if a strong electric current were constantly flowing through my body.

After the metal press had compressed all the cars, the train started to move faster. Even after it had departed the camp site, I was still frightened. The ride was rough and I feared the piece of coal that sustained my life was going to crumble any minute, turning all my efforts and struggle into nothing. As time passed, I was also increasingly tormented by suspicion. What if my friend betrayed me and told the guards that I had escaped by hiding in the train? Would he inform them, hoping to receive more food or be transferred to a safer work site? Prisoners did everything possible in order to get more food and a safer place to work. There were frequent accidents in the mine shaft, and seeing dead bodies carried out of the underground tunnel was part of the daily ritual. This would make any mining prisoner want to work elsewhere. But would he really do it? No way, I thought. The guards would know that I could not have lifted the heavy metal panel by myself. There had to be a collaborator. And if they found out that it was my co-worker, he would surely be executed. When the guards found out that I was missing, they might interrogate my friend, which would involve torture and even more starvation. He could prevent this by telling the truth in advance. In hindsight, my friend completely sacrificed his chance of survival for my sake, but at that moment, I could not help worrying about his fidelity.

It was awful to constantly imagine that they could stop the train any minute and drag me out. Every time the train slowed down, I felt like I was going to lose my breath. The worst moment was when the train stopped at the West Pyongyang Station for three to four hours. Having traveled all over the country for many years on business trips, I knew clearly where I was. The train had traveled southwest of Camp No. 18, the opposite direction of where I ultimately had to reach, that is, the border between Korea and Russia or Korea and China. However, most cargo trains had to pass through West Pyongyang, which was not a passenger station but a shipment depot located at a crossroads for many routes, wherever their final destinations were. There railroad workers spent hours checking cargo and train wheels. Even though I was aware of this, when the train did not move for so long, I was almost certain that they were searching for me. I flinched even more. Then I remembered a dream I'd had the night before my escape. In it I was a little child standing in a field full of chestnuts. I wanted to move, but I was barefoot. I did not know where my shoes were and I could not move an inch, not knowing what to do. Now in reality I felt the same desperate confusion. I knew that I had to get out of the car when the train stopped, but I had to do it in a secluded rural station in pitch darkness. Pyongyang was too crowded and it was not completely dark on the tracks, so I did not plan on escaping there. But when I thought the search was going on, I almost felt like taking the risk. Finally the train started moving again, and I knew that I had to get out at the next station for sure. The train in which I was hiding clearly displayed that its final destination was Muncheon, a town in Gang-won province, located nearby where I had worked in my youth. I knew the town well, but it was too far from the border. Go-on, a quiet railroad town at the border of South Pyeong-an and South Hamgyeong provinces, would be a better place to get off, since from there I could catch a train to Cheongjin, where I had a very close friend to ask for help. But even if I did not succeed in getting off at Go-on station, there was no reason to panic because I knew there was a direct line between Muncheon and Go-on that I could hide in. While these thoughts were competing in my head, I knew that they were only thoughts and the future had a mind of its own. I had no control over it and had to go as chance guided me.

Around 4:00 a.m. the train arrived in Go-on. It was dark, as there were not many searchlights. Even though Go-on was a small town, it bordered many provinces and many railways intersected there. This meant that the train would be stopped long enough for me to escape. The railroad workers checked the wheels of the train to see if everything was all right. I heard them talking to one another in a distinctive local accent when they passed by the car I was hiding in. I planned to catch a train to Cheongjin, where my old friend G from Revolutionary School lived. He was one of the friends who had traveled from Pyongyang to Cheongjin after we graduated. Since relocating required the official endorsement of the local government or the party, not many North Koreans moved their residence at will. So I was sure that he would still be in the area.

I crawled out of the train and could not move for several minutes because my joints were numb. I lay in silent pain beside the track. But it was dangerous to hang around too long at the railroad station, even though it was pitch dark outside. So I crawled and dragged myself gradually to a riverbank far from the railroad and sat down on the ground. I started to look for dry grass to clean my face, but I could not rub too much because my entire face was covered with all sorts and sizes of pimples due to malnutrition and lack of exposure to the sun. There was a full moon that night, and the river reflected the bright, indifferent moonlight. I could see my reflection clearly, down to every blemish and every contour of my distorted face. I was completely black from head to toe. On the moving train, the wind had blown through the hole and coated my face and body with soot, turning me into a monstrous creature that hardly looked human. I sat there under the moonlight and cried. Tears would not stop running down my face. I had never cried so hard during my six years of imprisonment, but now my emotions erupted all of a sudden. I asked myself how different life would have been if I hadn't been subjected to six years in the camp. How did all this happen, and why?

Having let out my emotions, I again began to move quickly. I washed my face in the river and started to search for clothes to wear. I still had my prisoner's dark gray uniform on and had to find civilian clothes as soon as possible. I saw some huts nearby and could see that there were clothes hanging outdoors. The air was cold and dry in late autumn, and many people left their lice-infested clothing outside so that the pests would freeze. The only problem was that there were dogs everywhere. If I were to get near those huts and one dog started barking, all the others would follow suit. I finally made up my mind to risk going back closer to town. There was simply no way to avoid the barking dogs. So I went back to the train station, where there was a dormitory for railroad workers nearby. It was still and quiet, but there might be hidden eyes watching me. As I expected, there were railroad workers' uniforms hanging outside the dorm on a rope, but even in darkness, I could see that they were ragged, with patches all over. Of course the workers would not leave their better uniforms outside for someone to steal. I quickly grabbed a complete uniform and found a pair of padded winter shoes and ran back to the remote area. My legs were shaking with weakness, but I was swift and quiet in my movements. The ragged uniform was all I needed and I felt lucky to get hold of it. When I took my prisoner's uniform off, there was a full layer of coal soot on my entire body. I washed it off with water, put on the railroad worker's uniform. I dug with bare hands and rocks at the hard frosty ground and buried the camp uniform. Only then—only then—I became overwhelmed by intense gratitude toward my friend who had let me take the chance to escape. I kept frantically saying to myself, *What could I do for you, what would you do to escape, what could I do, what would you do?* My entire body shook as if I were possessed. His timid eyes were still watching me from the darkness of the shaft where the coal train was parked. He was asking me to get into the car in a sorrowful voice. Tears soaked my face again and my heart was filled with regrets that he could not be here with me. I cried out that he had to be still in the darkest hell so that I could be here now.

Much later, I learned through some peddlers who go back and forth between China and Pyongyang that my friend who had helped me escape died of hunger in No. 18. Since he was a relatively influential figure in Pyongyang politics, the guards must have told someone in Pyongyang and the news reached the peddlers. As I think about it now, my friend was in frail condition but was among the stronger prisoners. To this day, I seriously doubt that he starved to death. There must have been some other reason. It tears me to pieces when I think about how he must have collapsed and gasped for his last breath under savage hands, never to see the outside world again.

In 1999, the North Korean economy was absolutely devastated. Due to extreme energy shortages, the trains ran slowly and irregularly, if they ran at all. Oftentimes a train would stop in the middle of nowhere due to lack of fuel. If this happened in the middle of winter, freezing passengers would pull out seats—whether they were upholstered seats from first class or simple wooden ones from the second and third classes—and burn them in the fields to stay warm. Therefore the passenger trains were gutted, as if there had been some rough raids. The timetables at the station did not mean anything and passengers had to stick around to catch anything that came by. Now that I was wearing "normal" clothes, I would invite less suspicion. But I did not have any money, so a cargo train looked like a better idea than a passenger train. Not only me, but any passenger frustrated with waiting would hop onto a cargo train without paying. There would often be violent altercations between free riders and train conductors, but those scenes were nothing out of the ordinary in those days.

While waiting in Go-on station, wearing the railroad worker's uniform, I saw a PRC-made military truck drive into the waiting area. My heart dropped. The truck looked like a patrol car deployed to arrest me, and I quickly hid behind the wheels of the nearest train parked at the station. The truck stopped and its occupants got out and began loading the bodies scattered around the station. I thought those were weary passengers who had fallen asleep while waiting for any train to pass by, but the bodies did not respond when they were thrown onto the truck like bags of garbage. When I was arrested and sent to camp in 1993, the situation in North Korea was bad, but it wasn't as ghastly as in 1999. In penal labor camps prisoners were well aware of what was happening in the outside world and politics, even more so than the people in society, because any big shots fallen out of favor would be sent to join us. But even though I knew that people were suffering from starvation, I did not expect death to be so prevalent, making life at the camp not so different from life in the world beyond the barbed wire. Later I heard that many orphans and homeless people flocked to train stations for shelter from the cold, but were driven out by station workers who want to avoid any responsibility. Late at night the homeless and orphans came back anyway and many ended up dead of cold and starvation, so it had become a ritual that at dawn a patrol truck carried away the piles of unmoving bodies on the floor of the waiting area, dead or not.

When I hopped onto the next cargo train going in the direction my close friend lived, I ran into some people who looked not too different from me. Because the cargo train transported coal and the blowing wind covered passengers' faces with soot, everyone was dirty. Everyone looked famished and jaded, just like the prisoners I'd left behind. At first I was relieved that I did not stand out among the crowd, but the more I observed, the sadder I became. How had our homeland become so devastated? I remembered the excursions I'd taken as a child in the orphanage and the Revolutionary School. We traveled by train and visited many revolutionary sites. The trains were clean and pleasant then, which made us children look forward to the next ride. What I was seeing now was a rotten corpse of the train from my childhood memory.

My mind was racing at the speed of the aged locomotive. I leaned against the shaking wall of the car and started to think about what I needed to do. As I'd worked in the National Security Agency before my arrest, I knew that if I crossed the Duman River to the Chinese side within a week of my escape, I would be safe. It would take that long for the agency to distribute my photo for a national search. Unlike elsewhere in the world where a computer network could transmit my image within seconds, in North Korea, if the NSA wanted to issue an all-points bulletin for me, they would have to print tons of photos and distribute them by truck. Plus, I knew well that if a prisoner disappeared from a penal labor camp, the checkpoints were closed and the guards started searching inside the camp. After all, it was really impossible to run away from there, so when prisoners went unaccounted for, it often turned out that they had committed suicide or died in accidents.

If the search inside the camp yielded no results, only then would a search outside the camp begin. The camp officials would call border security, inform them of the missing prisoner, and wait for an all-points-bulletin search to be approved by the NSA. It took about fifteen days from the moment camp authorities started an outside search to the moment photos had been distributed nationwide. This meant I would have roughly twenty days to flee North Korea after leaving the camp. I had long since calculated my time line while contemplating escape. Now that I had done it, my clock started ticking. I knew I did not have much time. But in order to continue, I had to get some help and replenish my energy. Since leaving the camp, I had eaten nothing. In such condition, I would collapse on the road. So I had to get to Cheongjin as soon as possible.

Old Friends

By North Korean standards, my friend G was relatively well off. He had worked for a chemical factory and headed the department in charge of transporting medicine throughout Northern Hamkyeong province for twenty years. All the medicine and medical equipment had to go through his department to be distributed to anyone—high or low in social standing, rich or poor, old or young—in the province. When international organizations donated medicine or medical equipment, it all went to a warehouse in Hoe-ryeong that stored war supplies. G was also in charge of that warehouse. He would distribute medicine with close expiration dates to military hospitals and then restock from new supplies of donated materials, mostly from the United Nations, in the warehouse. The goods piled up in there rarely went to the people who needed them.

G had access to pure alcohol, which he diluted with water and other drinks to make spirits. He would present this blend to bribe local party members to secure favors or sell it in the marketplace for cash. So even though his job was not a high-ranking position, he wielded power like a party official and was generally on good terms with the townspeople.

Back in the Revolutionary School days, we had been very close, and we became even closer after we joined the volunteers' group to work on the port construction in Cheongjin. Then we were so young and enthusiastic, greatly concerned with how to reassure our father, the Great Leader Kim Il-sung, about the project. Soon after we arrived in Cheongjin, G fell in love. The girl was a beauty who had also recently come to town as a film projectionist. Among 1,500-odd men, there were only 100 women working on the construction project. Most of them worked in cafeterias and stores, but no matter who they were and what they did, there was huge competition to get a date with any of them. But despite such an unequal gender ratio and the subsequent popularity any girl enjoyed, the film projectionist stood out as elegantly as a snow-white crane among the others. It was impossible not to have noticed her. G had to act fast if he wanted to get her, but the competition was too stiff. As a close friend, I decided to assist my friend's dating efforts and deterred everyone else from approaching her. Once I'd terrorized the potential suitors, I moved on to act as a matchmaker between the two. Soon after, the girl became pregnant and they got married. She was 21 and he was only 19. Every time I visited the couple, we had a fabulous time together. Even after I left Cheongjin for Kim Chaek Technological Institute in 1970, I remained a close friend and even a family member. The couple had twin boys who played Ping-Pong so well that they often visited Pyongyang for national matches. They always stayed with me and regarded me as an uncle. When they served in the military in their twenties, they would often visit me and take home all kinds of goods for their superiors or their own consumption. So I was convinced that I could trust G's wife while hiding in their house.

From 1988 to 1990, I had worked on another port construction project in the Rajin-Seonbong area, which bordered the Russian town of Khasan at the far northeast end of the Korean peninsula and was supposed to receive lumber that North Korean laborers sent from Siberia. There I had a chance to work with my friend again. At a glance, I could see that he was financially struggling. So I presented his family with a new TV set and a sewing machine, which were highly coveted items in North Korea;

this was probably equivalent to giving someone a new car as a present elsewhere. He was so grateful that he wanted to give me whatever cash he had, but I refused to take any money from a friend. He said he would not forget it, and he kept his promise. When he saw my indescribably tortured face and body in rags on his doorstep, he must have realized instantly that I was in deep trouble. But he did not ask me any questions. I simply told him that I had been unlucky with the auditors at my workplace. He said nothing. I did not tell him about the camp, because everyone in North Korea knew that prisoners simply did not escape from there. Although he was an extremely close friend, I would be asking too much if I asked him to protect a political prisoner who was on the run.

For slightly more than a week, he and his family took care of me as best as they could, making me feel comfortable and serving me food so that I could recover some strength. But like everywhere else in North Korea, everyone was watching one another, so there would be visitors from the leaders of the neighborhood committee. During the time I was hiding at his place, there were a couple of visitors. G emptied his closet and let me hide in it whenever they came. I crawled into a tiny space like I had in the train and silently waited for them to leave. G often took the guests to the opposite side of the room so that they would not detect my presence by any chance. While I was hiding at G's I thought about what my next move would be. Time was running out, and I had to make a decision soon. After much contemplation, I decided to escape to Russia. Back when I worked in the National Security Agency, I had been to Russian towns across the border a few times to sign trade documents, so I was familiar with the region. By the time the all-points-bulletin search was about to be issued, I had decided to go again to Rajin-Seonbong. The area was a special economic zone, and entrance required a special permit. Since G was the head of the distribution department, he had one. He visited several times a month and knew most of the security guards at the checkpoints. The guards asked him favors, to get them all kinds of medicines and vitamins, every time he drove by. G let me hide in a tank that he would load with carbide in Rajin-Seonbong. It was a three-hour drive from Cheongjin. I breathed through a rubber pipe attached to a gas mask I was wearing. G had secured it from a warehouse where medical supplies were stored. I gasped for air, but more importantly, I was cautious not to be detected by security guards who checked the truck twice on the road. Hiding in the tank was a good idea since it was marked with red letters indicating DANGER, EXPLOSIVE MATERIALS, and no guards bothered to check inside. We departed at night, and by the time we had passed all the security checkpoints and arrived in the border region, it was pitch dark. G stopped the truck by the Duman River and let me out of the tank. Before our departure he had given me a survival kit consisting of 6 pounds of dried cornmeal, 500 *won*,[1] a military flask made of rubber filled with drinking water, cough medicine, and a breathing tube for swimming across to Russia.

But the river that divided North Korea and Russia turned out to be wider than I had imagined, and the water temperature in November was too cold for anyone to swim. It was on the verge of freezing. So I had to change plans and go to Unggi, a rural town close to the Sino-Korean border. I would wait there until the water froze and I could cross on the ice. G led me to another mutual friend of ours named W. The three of us had become very close when working on the port construction project. One time we found a floating radio sent from South Korea and together we listened to a South Korean radio program. This was illegal and dangerous, and we made a pledge to keep it among us. Since that episode we had been friends who shared a secret. W also asked me no questions when he saw me. He lived in a border town, so it must have been obvious why I had to travel all the way up to the Sino-Korean border. I could not tell him of my plans, nor could he ask me about them. As a close friend, he was determined to help me no matter what the circumstances were, and it was easier not knowing the details. As old friends reunited, the three of us sat down together at W's dilapidated house, which looked more like a hut. We drank and wept bitterly that night. We celebrated our good memories and wept at the possibility of not seeing one another again.

"No matter what happens in the future, I promise I won't betray you. I cannot promise anything else, but I will never betray you," I told them, swallowing tears.

"I also promise not to betray you."

"I won't betray you either."

In our hearts, we were back to the old days when we were closer than brothers tied by blood, but our circumstances were about to separate us forever. We could not say anything further but wept all night.

For three days I stayed at W's house. Like most North Koreans in 1999, W was poor. He made his living by raising pigs and selling them to the government for corn, on which his entire family survived. Because famine was prevalent in North Korea, he could not leave the pigsty unguarded at night, so in addition to putting three large locks on the gate, he built a small room under the roof and above the sty and slept there every night, away from his family, guarding the only source of his livelihood. I volunteered to guard the pigs while hiding and spent three nights there. But I could not stay at his place too long. Even though it was a rural area with a small population, for that precise reason, I could be easily spotted. So I bid farewell to W and headed out toward the uncertain future.

Uninvited Guest

Soon after leaving W's house, I bumped into an old acquaintance on the street. I had met him some thirty years before, in 1970, when we belonged to the same military sports team. Despite the long years that separated us, we recognized each other immediately. He was glad to have run into me and told me that he was earning hard currency in a trading department for the military unit in the region. This was the kind of job I used to have before my downfall. I was more concerned than glad to have been recognized by him. Although I was wearing the clothes that G had given me, I was still a runaway prisoner desperately seeking to escape. It did not take long for him to notice signs of illness and anxiety on my face.

"What brings you to this area?" he asked me with great concern.

"I have been gravely ill lately and came here to seek medical treatment while staying with a friend," I replied slowly. I hadn't anticipated having to give such an explanation to anyone, so I had to say the first thing that came to my mind. Although I was wearing the military coat and trousers my friends had given me, I still must have looked terribly weak and ill from my days at the camp. I was glad that he seemed to believe what I said.

"Then let's go to my friend's house and ask for help. He is a good fellow who can help you with anything. His wife is a good friend of my wife."

I refused, but he was persistent. After a few more refusals, I gave in because he was genuinely trying to help and I was afraid that turning him down would only invite suspicion.

So unwillingly, I followed him to see his local friend, who was the vice-director of the Rajin-Seonbong Maritime Department. He held the rank of lieutenant colonel in the navy. His wife, whose name was L, was the political instructor for the family members of the local military personnel. My friend presented me as a foreign-currency earner from Pyongyang, which naturally made a favorable impression on the couple.

"So what brings you here to this remote area?" the husband asked.

"Well, I've fallen gravely ill and I am seeking medical treatment. And also there are some things I want to sell."

I had prepared this answer as my newfound acquaintance led me to this house. This explanation would pass the test because everyone knew that people with the right connections could obtain advanced medical treatment in China, although such travel was nominally forbidden for most North Koreans. In addition, the Rajin-Seonbong area was a special economic zone where trade between China and North Korea took place liberally, as many Chinese and Korean-Chinese merchants came there and crossed the border to trade. So did North Koreans, in order to sell their merchandise in China. Such border crossings were prohibited, but everyone did it in order to survive and supplement their meager income.

"Oh, what is it that you want to sell?" the husband replied with a sparkle in his eyes.

"I have some small but valuable pieces of Korean celadon."

"Ah, they are very popular in China." He seemed satisfied with this answer.

"If that's the case, I can help you sell your stuff. I have so many connections in the market on both sides of the border," his wife chimed in.

L, as she was called, was a charming woman full of energy and ideas. She was a typical political educator—very outgoing, eloquent, and persuasive.

"That's a good idea. We also have some celadon we want to sell in China," said her husband. He seemed to trust me completely. Indeed, what I said was nothing extraordinary since many Koreans went to China to sell celadon, as its price was far higher on the other side of the border. I was relieved to see the possibility of receiving their aid to cross into China emerge so openly and naturally. Because the mutual friend who had led me to their house was very close to the couple, the husband and wife seemed to have no doubts at all.

L suggested that I carry some of her merchandise and also promised to pair me up with an experienced guide who had crossed the border many times. I gladly agreed and thanked them for their help. They must have been doing their best to get on friendly terms with me, as I was supposed to be a high-flying NSA officer from Pyongyang who could return the favor when they needed it. The couple urged their children to introduce themselves to me and also treated me to a meal. I was grateful but felt increasingly uncomfortable playing a dangerous imposter game. So as soon as the meal was over, I took their small celadon, which I promised to sell together with my imaginary pieces in China. The couple invited me to stay longer at their place, but I absolutely did not want to linger. So I persistently asked them to take me to the final destination in North Korea, from which China was within a hand's reach.

Long Shadow on the Icy River

L's guide was a seasoned navigator of the border area who had some relatives on the Chinese side. He claimed that he constantly traveled between Rajin-Seonbong and Yanji,[2] a Chinese town where many ethnic Koreans lived. He had relatives there and was on his way to see them. The three of us rode a truck from Unggi to Namyang. The ride took less than an hour, but there were many checkpoints, which could have presented a huge problem had I not traveled with the group. L, who knew all the post guards in the area, could easily obtain their trust. It looked as if she traveled this route quite frequently. Having escorted us to the very far end of Korea, unsuspecting L went back to her home. I was thankful to my old friends who'd given me some cash to pay for the ride. In 1998, many trucks transported hungry North Koreans who were in search of food, so it was easy to mingle with them. Had it been the 1970s, when North Korean society functioned according to strict rules, it would have been much more difficult to cross the border.

In Namyang, my guide and I hid in caves in the mountains for about ten days until the Duman River froze. It took longer than he had anticipated, and what little dried corn my friends had packed for me would run out very soon, so we allowed ourselves very strict portions to get by. Still, toward the end of our hiding period, the dried corn ran out and all we could eat was snow. I was still in terrible health, but was somewhat assured that my guide had much experience in this. However, I did not trust him completely, and we talked very little while hiding. He only kept mumbling in a low, disgruntled voice that he needed to see his relatives sooner rather than later and that this crossing has taken longer than he'd expected. It was early December. Unlike on the Russian border, the river here was narrow and therefore easier to cross. I did not want to look suspicious in case I encountered other people, so I found a piece of broken glass in the mountains and shaved the beard on my face, reflected on the river. Although I'd replenished some energy at my friends' place, I was struggling. The severe conditions I had endured for six years in two camps had left many scars on my body, but they also trained me to withstand perpetual hunger. When a body experiences prolonged extreme hunger, the anus loses the ability to contract itself. When we were hiding in the mountains, I had been starved for so long that two fists could easily have been inserted into my anus. That's how weak my body was, but my mind was focused on one thing—successful escape. Even though I felt delirious at times, I could not afford to let my mind ramble. I had made it this far against all odds, but it would have been impossible if my friends had not taken enormous risks. All their sacrifices for my sake could be for nothing if I lost concentration even for a second.

We did not stay in one cave too long for fear of being discovered. It was easier to be on guard during the daytime, but at night we could not sleep long. The guide and I took turns standing vigil. But one sunny day while the guide was sleeping, I could not resist sleep any longer, so I came out of the cave and took a nap in the sun. It was a comforting feeling. But soon I heard voices nearby and immediately got up. I heard children's voices and discovered that a family was gathering wood chips for fuel. Luckily I had a bundle of tree branches with me, which I was going to burn in case it got too cold. As soon as I saw them, I got up, took the bundle, and walked away. The family did not pay too much attention, since there were many people who had to pile up fuel for harsh winter days. After that, I always carried the bundle, a useful prop for disguise.

The first snow fell around dusk in late December. As I looked at the pure snowflakes, my heart beat faster, as if the snow was some divine messenger signaling the portentous moment of my departure. But there were still guards along the riverbank. They weren't many, but the guide and I studied their movements carefully. We wondered if extra guards were hiding somewhere to capture escapees, but could not move around freely to find out. I could only hope that the guards I saw were the only ones. I had to take a chance or nothing would come of it. The guide noticed that the guards went to their posts around 7:30 p.m. for a very short shift. The river must be frozen by now; I was hoping that the ice was thick enough to support my frail body. At that place, the width of the river dividing North Korea from China was only twenty yards. The guide suspected that it was safe to make a move that evening. So when the time for the guards to change shift approached, I tied my shoes around my waist, massaged my strained legs with frozen fingers, and came down the hill to the riverbank. My feet were scratched and torn from the rough surface of the hillside. I carried two long canes in case the ice broke. I planned to use them to climb out of the icy water just like I had learned in the revolutionary history class at school. Kim Hyoeg-gon, Kim Il-sung's uncle, had also carried two canes when crossing the thin ice of the Duman River while fighting the Japanese colonialists. He was running away from the foreign aggressors to save his homeland; now I was running away from my own people to save myself. Ironic as it may be, the revolutionary history that we'd studied so diligently in school became a guiding light at a moment when I was looking for any assurance and assistance in escaping with my life.

It must have taken less than three minutes to cross the river, but it felt more like three hours. For fear of losing any split second, I never looked back while on the ice and steadily focused my gaze at the dark bank of the Chinese side. My entire body was charged with unbearable tension. I can still hear and sense my rough heartbeat. I wasn't paying any attention to the guide who accompanied me. Instead of walking, I was sliding carefully across. The guards were still at their posts and did not see us. Only after I'd reached the Chinese side did I notice that the guide had also managed to cross without trouble. A sensation overcame me that I was in a relatively safe place for the first time since the escape. But that feeling of relief did not last too long, because there were Chinese border guards on this side. If they caught me, they could easily send me back to North Korea. I looked around and saw only ten households, a road, and a mountain beyond. It was the first time I'd set foot in China, and I had no idea where I was. The guide whispered that it was better to split up than to hang around together, since it was easier for one person to find a hiding spot than for two. He had already given me the phone number of his relatives in Yanji, so he urged me to call if something happened. I entrusted him with L's celadon pieces and asked him to sell them for me, since I was not planning to return to Unggi. He took the little treasures and promptly disappeared. I was at a loss. Soon after, dogs started barking frantically. I heard a car approaching and immediately hid myself in the bushes. It was Chinese police. My heart sank. I waited in silence until they passed by. As soon as the car disappeared from sight, I went out on the road again. Then I saw the car turn and come back in my direction. I climbed up the foothills of the mountain and decided to hide and observe the situation. The police patrol went back and forth along the same road and finally left.

When I came down from the hills, it was freezing. I was wearing shabby clothes that were not appropriate for harsh winter days. I looked around and spotted a red brick building with a cross on the roof at the edge of the village. I had no choice but to go there; wandering around on the street would be asking for arrest. I hurriedly moved toward the red brick building and snuck into a boiler room where I could warm myself. Having hidden in the cold mountain hills for ten days, I felt overwhelming warmth when I closed the door. The warmth of this indoor space was so embracing that I felt like it could melt me. For a short moment, I could almost forget that I was still in great danger. But before I could get completely lost in reverie, I was discovered by an elderly worker. He was a kind-looking man who seemed to have guessed what my circumstances were. He spoke to me in Korean with a strange accent.

"No safe here. No safe. The police find soon. They come. Can't stay."

He spoke in broken Korean, but there was no problem following what he meant. I must be in a town of Korean-Chinese people. This was good news, because I could at least communicate with them. Later I learned that the village where I arrived in China was called Tumen.[3] The kind-looking man with the thick accent led me to another building nearby. He took me to the back storage room in a restaurant kitchen, where I hid for five days. There I could at least avoid frostbite and eat garbage from the kitchen. I had practically starved in the mountains for many days and was extremely weak. In a large metal bin, there were half-eaten apples, fried rice, bits of vegetables, all floating in gooey and scummy liquid. I dug into the garbage and ate anything I could find. At night I ventured out to the courtyard and looked for cigarette butts on the ground. I could find some half-smoked ones and lit them with matches given me by my friends in North Korea. They tasted heavenly. As I was inhaling the tobacco smoke to my last breath, I thought of my friends. I must go farther away so that I could be safer. If I were caught and sent back to North

Korea, it would also mean great danger for them. I should not let them down. Being in Tumen was so much better than hiding in the mountains, but I was afraid that the Chinese police might find me at any time.

The kind man had a wife who was a churchgoer. She came to see me in the hiding place on the fourth day. She also brought me a lunch box and clothes to wear.

"You will stand out if you keep wearing those clothes. Anyone will know you are a North Korean escapee. Better change into these." She recommended that I go to a church where I could meet missionaries who would help me escape.

Next day she brought a South Korean couple along and told me that they were Christian missionaries. I was taken aback by falling into South Koreans' hands. I felt anxious, as my plan—although I did not know how to realize it—was to go to Japan eventually, where I could ask for help from the business partners I had befriended while working at the NSA. But my situation was too precarious and I was not able to get any farther from North Korea on my own. So I had no choice but to tell the couple that I was an escapee who could not return to the north and ask for their help. The couple did not inquire further, but even if they had, I was not going to tell them anything else about myself. Once again, my life depended on complete strangers' mercy.

Across the Continent 6

Still on the Border

The missionary couple led me to a Korean Chinese worker couple's household in Yanji and gave me US$230 as an emergency fund. My hosts worked all day in town, so they had me hide in a room and gave me both food and a bucket that I could use as a toilet. By the time they returned home from work, the entire room reeked. I felt embarrassed handing the bucket over to them to take out and empty. In an effort not to embarrass me further, they said nothing at those moments. They seemed to be close to the South Korean missionary couple and silently took it as their duty to host me, which must have presented some risk to them. But I could not relax by any means. I couldn't afford to trust anybody too much. Why were the South Koreans so generous with their help? What could they get out of it? I wondered if they had any hidden motivations. Could they be South Korean agents posing as missionaries, trying to capture me off guard? Or even worse, could they be working for Chinese police who wanted to collaborate with North Korean authorities searching for escapees? There was no way to find out, as this couple was my only connection to the world. At the same time, I also felt extremely grateful to them for doing their best to keep me safe. While I was hiding there, I had nothing to do but think. All sorts of plans and thoughts came and went fleetingly, but after a while, my mind fluctuated between two extremes: feelings of gratitude would quickly be replaced by suspicion, which then would be clouded over by feelings of gratitude. The process would repeat itself until one of the couple came into the room to interrupt my thoughts.

While hiding in that house, I saw my mother in a dream. I was on a platform at a train station, waiting for her to show up. She did not come and I became nervous. The next moment, I was on a train and she was sitting next to me. She was wearing snow-white traditional dress and shoes. She looked so relaxed. The train was crammed and I felt stifled, but she kept saying, "My goodness, it is so comfortable here, it is like heaven." A conductor entered our train and started to check tickets. I got nervous and started looking everywhere in my pockets without finding a ticket, but my mother, still very relaxed, handed a clean white paper to the conductor. When he unfolded it, her name was written vertically in Chinese characters. He looked at it and said, "Very good, have a good trip." When I woke up, my face was covered with warm tears. I hoped that Mother had had a good trip to the netherworld, just like I had seen in my dream. I wished that she would rest peacefully there without any further suffering. But as for me, I still had a long way to go. The nervous feelings I had in the dream carried over into real life, as I was traveling without a ticket and the train was taking me to an unknown destination.

Yanji

My stay with the Korean-Chinese couple reached its limit, and the South Korean missionaries, whom I now thought of as Mr. and Mrs. M, led me to a clean, empty apartment. It was a small two-bedroom on the fifth floor in a residential area on the outskirts of Yanji. By this time, I'd come to trust the couple a bit more, so before they left me in the new shelter, which was filled with food and Christian books, I asked them if they could deliver a note to the border guide who had accompanied me. They gladly agreed. I asked them to call the guide, who was staying with his relatives in the same town, and also handed over the money they'd given me, for him to deliver to L. I wrote another letter saying that, due to my health, I thought it would take some time to sell the celadon pieces, so instead of keeping them, I'd entrusted them to the guide. I concluded the letter by urging L to come to China herself to expedite the process. As I was not sure if the guide could fulfill the couple's expectations of selling their celadon, I felt quite uneasy and wanted to show them that I had not vanished with their treasures. Mr. and Mrs. M quietly observed me handing over all the emergency money I had, so when they received it together with the letter and note, they left more emergency money.

When the couple left me in the new apartment, they locked the door from the outside. I could hear the metal lock click sharply. The sound painfully reminded me of Camp No. 14, where they locked the prisoners in at night. Mr. and Mrs. M told me that it was for my own safety, but it made me incredibly uneasy. The couple kept coming almost every day to replenish food and other supplies for my comfort. As I observe them religiously coming and going, I kept thinking, *Are they telling me the truth about helping me to reach a safer place? Or are they buying time until the North Korean authorities arrive to arrest me?* At the very beginning of my stay in that apartment, I seriously thought of killing them and setting myself free. I often thought of various ways to do it and contemplated for hours about which weapon would serve my purpose the best. There were kitchen knives and hammers in the apartment. I could hide behind the door when they entered and stab them or break their skulls. But whenever I saw them come and prepare meals for me, I felt such sincere kindness exuded in their words and deeds that I could not move myself to act. However, not having any connection to the outside world, I was growing impatient. I had to do something and be prepared to react in case of emergency. I started saving every single razor blade the couple gave me and broke them into tiny pieces. Then I dissolved cookies in water and made dough with broken blades in it. I made small balls out of the dough, dried them, and always kept them in my pocket. I planned to swallow them if I was arrested. Having gone through the worst kind of imprisonment on earth, I would have gladly swallowed the cookie balls without a second thought. Now that I was prepared for the worst-case scenario, I felt a bit easier.

In the first two weeks, the couple seemed to have noticed my strange, suspicious behaviors and to want to do what they could to earn my trust. That made me relax a little. A few weeks later, I bluntly asked them if they had delivered the note and money to the border guide in town.

"Yes, do you want to meet him in person?" the husband asked me calmly.

"Could, could I?" I asked in a trembling voice. I had spent roughly a month in that apartment, and my patience was wearing thin.

"If you wish, we could arrange a meeting in a teahouse, but we all have to be very careful, as there are plenty of Chinese police searching for North Korean escapees everywhere."

"Sure, sure. That would be good."

A few days later, the couple asked me to dress in clothes they'd brought from South Korea and accompanied me to a small teahouse in the evening. There was the border guide, who told me that he had received the money and the note to be handed over to L. He was still taking care of his business, but was planning to go back to North Korea soon. I repeatedly told the guard to tell L and her husband that it would be best if they came to China to sell the celadon themselves and that I was sending this money in the meantime. As I had virtually no mobility, I knew I could not fulfill L's expectations. I asked Mr. M if he could give me a phone number where L or her husband could contact me once they arrived in China. Mr. M gladly wrote down a number and gave it to the guide.

That turned out to be one of my two outings during six months of confinement in that apartment. Mr. and Mrs. M kept coming and told me to read the Bible and pray. I did not touch the Bible, which I'd never seen before. Nonetheless, the couple came at 5:00 a.m. and sat with me to offer early morning prayers. They also taught me how to pray. They never told me of future plans, which drove me insane. Whenever I looked impatient, they only asked me to pray sincerely. They also brought videotapes on the life of Jesus. Not having anything else to do and staying inside all day by myself, I sometimes watched them without much thought. One day, all of a sudden, the wife asked me how the Korean War had broken out.

"Of course, the American imperialists instigated the South Korean puppets to invade our brothers and sisters in the north." I answered nonchalantly the way I knew it.

"No, the fact is, on Sunday, June 25, 1950, when most military forces were off guard, Kim Il-sung launched a sneak attack on South Korea. Because it was a sneak attack, the North Korean invaders could quickly force their way down to the far southern city of Busan in three days." The wife replied calmly, but she was unflinching in her manner.

Ideology was a strange thing—mysteriously addictive and stubbornly unchanging. I was arrested, tortured, and sentenced to slow death by hard labor by the North Korean regime, but at that moment, I could not help but feel offended that Mrs. M challenged what I believed to be historical truth. I did not refute this kind woman, but I felt she was insulting me by distorting what I firmly believed to be a fact.

Companion in Misfortune

One day Mr. and Mrs. M came early in the morning to tell me some news from North Korea. The wife told me that the previous night, she'd received a phone call from L. She called from Tumen, the first Chinese town I'd found after crossing the border. L was temporarily staying there and had no place to go, so I asked Mrs. M to let me meet her and explain the situation. So Mr. M took me to the Korean-Chinese couple's house where I'd stayed for five days, and Mrs. M brought L from Tumen to meet me. A month and a half had passed since we've seen each other in North Korea. So much had changed in her in that short period of time. She had been a confident and charming woman full of good will and energy. Now she sat in the dark room, all disheveled and disarrayed, not knowing where to start her story.

"I cannot believe what happened to me and my family . . . it's really hard to believe."

"So tell us what happened," I said impatiently, as I had an ominous feeling that I played a major role in her current misery.

"Well, after you left with the guide, we waited and waited to hear from you, and when more than two weeks passed, we decided to find out what was going on. I have a permit to travel to China, so I came to Tumen and took care of some business and looked for you or the guide. I stayed more than ten days, to no avail. I simply had to go back home because the local elections were approaching and given my job, it would be terrible to miss them. So I got back on the train to return to Namyang, North Korea . . . and guess what I saw there?" She was getting agitated and started to talk faster. Everyone listened nervously.

"I ran into a group of policemen who rounded up North Korean runaways in China. I see such scenes quite often, but this time among the arrested, there was the guide who accompanied you from Namyang to Tumen. When I saw him, I froze and turned my eyes away, but he saw me too. He was careful not to talk to me or show signs of recognition. But he kept staring at me and I secretively returned his gaze from time to time. It looked like there was something he wanted to say. Soon I noticed that he was signaling with his cuffed hands. They were pointing to his right pocket. I realized that he had something to pass on to me, but I was scared to death that the police might see us communicating and arrest me as well."

L stopped for a while and lifted her blank gaze.

"So what happened?" Mrs. M asked L, who still looked lost.

"Finally for a split second, one of the two police escorts went away, I don't know where. And the other turned his back to us. That's when the guide pulled a folded paper out of his pocket and made sure I saw it. I had to act quickly. I got up from my seat, walked by, and grabbed the white paper from his hand. Luckily no one saw us. I went to the next compartment, holding the paper tightly in my palms, and stood there for a while. I was shaking terribly. I did not move until the train arrived in Namyang. Only after I got off the train did I open the note and find some foreign money and a letter from you." She looked me directly in the eye.

"You can't imagine how nervous I felt then. You know what it means—to receive a letter from China like that, passed on by an illegal border crosser. Had the guide not gotten the letter to me and had it been discovered by the police in North Korea, that would have been a huge mess. So I tried to calm down and went back to the Rajin-Seonbong area, where the real surprise was waiting."

She stopped her story but kept staring at me with a hollow gaze, as if looking at a specter.

"There in my hometown, I saw your face everywhere. Everywhere on the street, in the public marketplace, on the walls of schools, they glued pictures of your face with a detailed description of your crime."

I lowered my eyes. I could not bear to meet her gaze. I knew it was about time the NSA issued an all-points bulletin, especially near the border area.

"I went straight home and found that nobody was there. A neighbor heard me and came over all flustered. She told me that my husband thought I was kidnapped by the criminal who had masqueraded as a Pyongyang official and that he, together with police, had gone to find out my whereabouts. In the meantime, this neighbor was going to take care of our children. I did not see my children because they were at school when I came home." L was noticeably trembling while she talked about her family. Nobody interrupted her this time.

"I knew what it all meant. It was all over for us. It was all over. . . . My husband was probably detained by the police despite his innocence, and they would arrest me in no time when they made up their minds that we had contacts with the worst criminal on the run. . . . I did not spend another second in my house after the neighbor left and went straight back to Namyang, and crossed the river on foot when darkness fell. When I arrived in Tumen, I called the number written on your note, and here I am."

I could not say anything for a while. I was listening to her story with a lowered head, not meeting her blank gaze. But soon I recovered my composure and said to Mr. and Mrs. M, "L is a relative of mine, and because she was helping me escape from North Korea, she and her family got into this huge trouble. I really don't know what to say, but may I please beg you to let her hide in the apartment with me? She cannot go back now, and if she got caught here, it would be terrible."

Mr. and Mrs. M did not object. They did not question what I said, but they wanted to know more about L, who was speechless after her long talk.

"Her husband is a vice director of the Maritime Department in Rajin-Seonbong," I started to help out. Mr. and Mrs. M showed great interest in what I had to say. They wanted to hear more about her background. Having perceived this positive signal, I went on.

"Quite an influential guy on the other side. L is also well connected, because she worked as a political instructor for the military families. She knows them all very well."

The couple was glad to know that this woman had a lot to tell about the other side of the border they could not approach. I sensed that they were sympathetic about her misery; in addition, L could be valuable for their own work of assisting refugees. In the middle of the night we all came back to the apartment where I was hiding and continued to talk. This is how I was joined by L, who never had expected that hosting an unknown guest so briefly and unsuspectingly could completely change her life.

During the six months of my stay, the couple brought three other escapees to the apartment. They were brought in sequence, but I was told not to interact with them.

"If the guest asks questions, just tell him that you are the owner of this house, okay?" the wife told me.

One of the guests told me that he was simply touring the area. But there was no deceiving each other. People on the run shared that sixth sense that could tell suspicion, uncertainty, and fear. Escapees could easily spot someone in the same situation. He later told me that he was a medical doctor from Cheongjin and was now helping the couple smuggle various medicines and first aid supplies back into North Korea. When I heard this, I felt scared that the couple and the doctor had some ties to North Korea. L was also afraid of the possibility. I still had suspicious moments about my precarious position. I modified my plans and decided to run out the front door if something went wrong. L, who was still in shock, agreed with me, and we reminded each other not to get completely relaxed.

But as vigilant as I was, deep in my heart, I was very much assured that the couple did not mean any harm. The wife would make warm meals every morning after prayers. She would mix various healthy grains with rice, and sometimes for lunch she would come back from a market with azalea-flavored noodles to stimulate my appetite. In the refrigerator, there were bananas, oranges, apples, and much more. She was really trying to restore my health with great care. Gorging on all kinds of appetizing food, I transformed from an emaciated skeleton into a fat pig. My belly started to bulge. I'd been subject to perpetual hunger for such a long time that everything tasted like honey, and I could not throw food away. I must have weighed less than 90 pounds in camp, but in six months at the apartment I put on an extra 55 pounds. Never had I thought of women in camp, but during those months of idling away, doing nothing but eating, I felt sexual desire for the first time since my arrest.

During this time of hiding, I often thought about my life in North Korea. Back in the days when I was working for the NSA and driving long hours, I set my radio to the South Korean channel in order to listen to music to stay awake. One time, I blasted South Korean music while driving with my superior D. D looked at me and asked what I was listening to. I told him that it was one of those foreign songs from a country of communist brotherhood and that it had been presented in this year's April Festival when more than 100 countries sent musicians to commemorate Kim Il-sung's birthday. D turned his squinting eyes toward me and said firmly, "Bullshit, it does not sound like it. You are bullshitting again." But in spite of critical remarks delivered in a severe tone, he did not switch the channel. He just kept listening to the song, betraying his intention to stay free of bad capitalist influence. It is no secret that the North Korean leadership was very familiar with South Korean popular culture. While searching for radio signals, at times, I would inadvertently end up listening to anti–North Korean propaganda programs broadcast by the South Korean radio station. They were mostly about the fallacies of Kim Il-sung's regime. The South Korean anchors said in their over-sweetened voices that the sufferings of the North Korean people were due to the Kim rulers' exploitation. I always laughed at such nonsense, but later in the camp, those South Korean radio comments came back to haunt me occasionally, which made me think how easy it had been for me to dismiss them when my life was following the model of the impeccably successful revolutionary heroes.

While hiding, I watched many South Korean TV dramas that the missionary couple brought. I felt a sense of alienation watching these stories of romance, jealousy, and love. Unlike characters in most North Korean dramas, which were about grandiose missions and ideas that transcended individuals, such as community, country, and socialist revolution, the South Koreans seemed to be immersed in their own individual problems. Male characters were shedding tears like women, which surprised me a great deal. L could not believe it either. But these men, as effeminate and ridiculous as they seemed, freely explored their own thoughts and feelings. I thought about whether I'd ever had a moment to really give special consideration to my close ones. My wife and children always came second to my devotion to our leaders and homeland. I did not think about my personal feelings and issues as much as the people on South Korean TV. I carried a party membership card wherever I went. It had Kim Il-sung's portrait on it, and by keeping it close to my heart I always felt physical love toward it.

The most memorable South Korean program I saw was one that arranged meetings of family members long separated by the Korean War. Even within South Korea itself, there were so many people who had been torn apart from their wives, husbands, brothers, and sisters during the war and were still living like strangers thirty or forty years after the cease-fire. The program featured a dying mother who could not recognize her middle-aged son, whom she had last seen as a toddler. Brothers and sisters would wail upon finding out that their parents had passed away without their knowledge. The same program sometimes would feature Korean orphans adopted by American families. After long years they came back to their homeland to search for their biological parents. While watching these incredible moments, a thought came to my mind. Mother had once told me about her uncle who lived in South Korea. Maybe I could find him through this channel! I quickly wrote down the contact number of the Korean Broadcasting System program producers in the back leaf of the Bible. I promised myself that as soon as I reached a safe place, I would call the number to reach out to this unknown uncle. I was greatly moved while watching these programs that gave me hope of finding a new family member in the south. But what about my family in the north? Warm tears streamed down my face, wetting my shirt, while my mind rushed through a series of questions. What were my wife and children doing? What had happened to them after my escape? Would I ever see them again?

L, who had very recently lost her family, sat and watched the program with me, sometimes crying silently, sometimes wailing out loud. She could not live with the fact that she had so easily left her children behind. Everything had happened so suddenly when she fled North Korea that she did not have any time to think about what would happen to them. At that moment, she was so afraid that if she lingered, someone would come to arrest her like so many others she'd witnessed. But poor children, they had committed no fault of their own! A terrible sense of guilt tormented her. She would have moments of outburst when she wailed and blurted out sentences broken by deep suffering.

"Even, even the wild beasts . . . even the beasts look after their babies! So much better! So much better than a human being like me . . . crazy and selfish human being like me . . . I am worse than the beasts! A million times worse!!!"

At these moments she insisted that she needed to go back to North Korea for the sake of the children. Although she knew there was nothing she could do for them, she had to release these thoughts aloud to relieve her pain. Was she really hoping that she could at least live with them in the camp like I did with my mother in Camp No. 18? As the culprit who'd ruined her family life, I suffered with her. That was the least I could do for her. I urged her to blame me openly if that made her feel any better. But instead, L eventually sought solace in reading the Bible and offering prayers as Mrs. M had taught her. Nevertheless, we often cried together, wiped each other's tears, and vainly consoled each other that we would see our lost family members soon. Through the repeated process of mourning and consolation, L and I became close confidants. Most times, there was nobody but us in the shelter, and we became companions sharing everything—the sense of imminent danger, anxiety about the future, loss, self-pity, and loneliness, which all fueled carnal desire to fill the unbearable void of life.

Beijing

In the sixth month of my stay in that Yanji apartment, when I'd almost fully recovered my bodily strength, what seemed like an eternal waiting period finally came to an end. Mr. and Mrs. M came to see L and me one day to announce our impending departure. The final destination was South Korea. The couple explained that they were searching for ways to get us there as soon as possible. It had become obvious that the South Korean embassy in Beijing would not accept us and grant us asylum. South Koreans simply wanted to avoid anything that might cause conflict with China. The couple had thought about sending us on a boat crossing the Yellow Sea between China and the Korean peninsula, but that turned out to be risky as well. They had recently heard that a North Korean diplomat stationed in Beijing had disappeared with his wife, and the North Korean police were on alert in the urban and port area near the city to look for them. So the idea of a short trip from the east coast of China to the west coast of Korea had to be abandoned. The missionaries concluded that we had no choice but to get to South Korea via Mongolia. Once we arrived in Mongolia, everything would be fine, according to their explanation. We could pose as South Korean tourists who'd gotten lost in the border area and ask the Mongolian authorities to send us to the South Korean embassy in Ulaanbataar.

It promised to be a long and dangerous journey. But Mr. and Mrs. M wanted to get us out of the Yanji apartment for fear that there might be a police raid if we stayed too long. They brought us well-prepared packages, which showed that they were constantly working to ensure the safest and easiest journey to South Korea. L and I became teary when we finally realized that we were about to bid farewell to the kind couple who had taken such good care of us. They read our minds, and their eyes also welled up. The couple made us wear everything South Korean from head to toe—underwear, outerwear, watches, shoes, backpacks, currency, and wallets. Everything we carried, except our counterfeit South Korean passports, was genuinely South Korean. The couple also gave us a large sum of money—1,500 U.S. dollars and 6,000 Chinese *yuan* for each person. I packed everything, including the Bible, which I've started reading during the past six months of hiding. I also carefully packed my "suicide balls" made of cookie dough and broken razor blades in case I was recaptured by the police and sent back to North Korea. Next morning, Mrs. M, L, and I departed for Beijing by train; we arrived at the capital city in the evening. Having been isolated from the bustling world for over seven years, I felt quite dazzled by the pandemonium of the train station in a large city. The sense of excitement was compounded by the danger of being captured by the Chinese police and repatriated at any moment. There was quite a bit of police presence at the station, and we did everything we could to ignore them. Mrs. M asked L and me to wait for her at the station while she tried out the bus route to Erenhot, a Chinese town in Inner Mongolia bordering Mongolia, to see how strict the security was. She thought that things would be safer once we reached Mongolia. L and I decided to stay there, amid the bustling crowd, rather than go into a quiet residential area in case something were to happen to us. However, when it approached 1:00 a.m., a police patrol went around the waiting area in the station and started to check people's ID. L and I panicked. We carried the counterfeit South Korean passports, but we could not tell how authentic they looked. So we hurriedly left the waiting area and were glad to see a woman holding a sign written in Korean: HOME STAY. We approached her and asked how much she would charge for the night. She answered in a typical Korean-Chinese accent that 100 *yuan* would do. Without a second thought, we let her lead the way through the tiny back streets near the station to a dilapidated apartment building. We spent the night there half asleep, half awake, then went back to the train station. We waited all day, but Mrs. M did not show up. When night fell, we went back to the same place as the night before. The hostess welcomed us again. The following morning, the third day of our stay in Beijing, we finally saw Mrs. M. We led her to the boarding house, and there we sat and talked about her expedition to the border area. She told us that it took a day and a half to get to Erenhot, the Chinese entry point to the Gobi Desert, and that the security checkpoints were not too strict. She thought it would be all right for us to travel there. The wife asked the hostess of the boarding house if she would escort us to Erenhot, since we didn't speak Chinese, and offered to pay 500 *yuan*. The easygoing woman agreed. Mrs. M also requested that she carry her husband's Chinese ID for me to borrow, just to be prepared for a thorough security check. The hostess easily agreed to this as well.

Mrs. M then told us to stay at the boarding house and went out to take care of some other business. She had just come from a long bus ride and looked very tired, but she was on her way again. Sometime later in the afternoon, she returned with a woman, another North Korean escapee who was to go to Mongolia with us. She was in her early forties and, like so many other North Koreans, had suffered immensely due to economic hardship. Her husband had died of liver disease a few years before in North Korea and she had no means to support her children. So she entrusted them to her parents and traveled to seek help from her husband's relatives, who lived in the very far northern region. She begged, but they had neither means to help nor sympathy for her. She gave up all hopes of surviving and threw herself in the Duman River. She nearly drowned, but fate did not allow her to die like that. Her floating body was discovered by Christian missionaries on the other side of the border and she was rescued. So without knowing it, she had crossed the border between Korea and China, death and life. After she recovered her health, she was brought to Beijing, just like us, to reach South Korea. She was in the same boat as we were, and we immediately became close.

The next morning, the four of us—Mrs. M, L, the new woman who had joined the party, and me—were again in the train station. This time, we were embracing one another and shedding tears. I thanked Mrs. M for the care she had given us. Were it not for this kind woman and her husband, what would have become of me? The other two women were also holding her hand and embracing her. The hostess of the boarding house also wiped her tears. Soon Mrs. M was standing outside the bus window and waving at us. We waved until she disappeared from sight, but before she did, she became a blurry figure, as my vision was clouded by tears.

The two-story bus smelled of all sorts of things—sweat, dust, gasoline, and smoked meat. It was packed with Mongolian merchants on their way home. We rode all day through the vast land, and the scenery changed as we drove out of the busy Beijing area into remote rural mountains and later to wide-open plain. The three women were chatting constantly like little girls going on a field trip, but I mostly remained silent, worrying about the security check. When night fell, as Mrs. M told us, we passed the checkpoint. We all kept silent. Before departing, we had agreed that if anybody asked us any questions, the hostess of the boarding house would reply to the security guards that we were tourists from South Korea. But the actual security check was quite cursory—a police officer got on the bus with a flashlight and stood right next to the driver's seat, randomly glancing at sleepy faces without bothering to walk down the aisle. That was all. As worried as I was about this part of the journey, I almost felt deceived when the officer got off the bus just like that. The next day at 4:00 p.m., we arrived in Erenhot. This was the last post of the vast Chinese land, a small town on the remote outskirts. We went to the inn recommended by Mrs. M. It was the middle of summer, and the heat was scorching. The four of us got a taxi to the marketplace. There we found a noodle shop run by Korean Chinese who spoke quite good Korean. The male host seemed to have guessed why we were there. The four of us had a very nice meal at this restaurant and ended up befriending him. For some reason, I felt like I could trust him; when we were about to leave, he pulled us aside and asked if one of the women could stay with them and help out with the restaurant business. He explained that they badly needed extra hands. We politely declined and in return asked if he could accompany us to the border the next day. He wrote down the address of our inn.

The hostess of the boarding house bid us farewell and went back to Beijing the next morning. It was August 27, 2000. I remember the date because it was L's birthday. We had a small party for her in the room where we were staying and decided that we'd better not do anything drastic or dangerous that day, according to Korean custom. So we stayed at the inn and listened to the raindrops hitting the window of our room. However, close to midnight, we heard a knock on our door. It was the host of the noodle shop. He told us that it hadn't rained so hard in the past three years and that this was the perfect night to cross the border. So we hurriedly packed and took a taxi to the very edge of Chinese territory. We could walk to Mongolia. According to the host, if we went all the way to the border at this place, the chances of being discovered by the patrol were greater, so he advised us to walk about two miles in the direction he pointed and we would be able to enter Mongolia without running into the guards. We all gave him a huge hug for his help. Now the three of us were left in the heavy rain. It was pitch dark and there was no trace of a human being. Nothing was to be seen or heard. We started to walk, each carrying a heavy backpack into desolate uncertainty. The destination was so near, but it was not visible in the thick darkness of rain.

Pillar of Fire

I don't know how long we walked on the muddy sand. Our socks and shoes were completely soaked in mud, which kept us from moving swiftly. Our bodies were dripping. The two women sometimes needed help, and I could see why Mr. and Mrs. M had sent us as a group. Although I'd been very close to death when I escaped North Korea, six months of care had restored my strength to lead and support two fellow travelers. We marched forward without talking. We all felt like we'd walked far more than two miles when we reached tall fences with barbed wire at the top. There they stood, about eight feet high, like a highlight of a spectacular journey. There were two rows of fencing not far apart. We all gasped for breath at that exciting moment. This was it! Without wasting a single minute, we threw our backpacks on the ground and I promptly bent down to make a stool for the two women to stand on so they could reach out and grab the top of the barbed wire. Then I got up and lifted them so that they could go over and land in between the two fences. When they were done, I threw all three backpacks to the other side and climbed over the fence myself. We repeated the same process for the second fence, and there we were in Mongolia. We were so excited that we did not notice how our clothes and skin had gotten torn when we grabbed the sharp wires with our bare hands. We were ecstatic as our cheeks, hands, and legs were bleeding from deep scratches. The rain had stopped by then, but the ground was as muddy as it could get. We kept walking and walking. We walked and talked. But our talking became rare as we kept going, because we started to wonder whether we would be able to meet anyone or anything on the road. I still cannot tell how much distance we covered after we crossed the two rows of fences. Our legs were deep in the mud and moving became increasingly difficult. When we'd just crossed the border, I was so ecstatic that I was not even aware of the big backpack on my back, but now that the excitement had slowly dissipated, I started to feel its weight. Soaked in rain, it felt heavier than ever. New anxieties started to emerge in our minds. Where were we? Why could we not find anything—shelter of any kind, any people? The night was vast and dark, not giving us any hint as to where we were heading. We did not have any plans about what to do in Mongolia. Even Mr. and Mrs. M had told us that everything would be fine once we got there. All of us had been so focused on our immediate goal—to escape China, where we could be sent back to North Korea—that nobody had envisioned this stage of our long journey.

Fear began to arise, but I did not speak of it. All I could hear was the heavy drops of rain falling onto the sandy desert again. About an hour after our border crossing, the two women started to talk to each other in low voices, wondering why they were walking endlessly without running into anything. This was the Gobi Desert, a name I'd only heard of when I studied geography in school a long time ago. Now I was leaving my footprints there, but before I completed my journey it could simply swallow me without any trace. Even in darkness, we could sense that there was really nothing on the far distant horizon. We were completely surrounded by the merciless vastness. Our legs were bleeding from scratches, but we did not waste any time putting bandages on, as we wanted to move as far away from China as we could. The night in the desert was chilly, especially under pouring rain for hours. As we marched forward, I could hear my teeth chatter. We could not see well due to the heavy showers. Our initial fear had been discovery by the border patrol, but now we were worried about not running into anyone. What if we had to walk for weeks in this wasteland? What if our provisions ran out? The emerging battle with nature started to overwhelm us and we increasingly looked downward as our strength ran low.

That was when I saw it. I lifted my eyes to fight gloomy thoughts and overwhelming fatigue and saw on the distant horizon a huge pillar of fire in a whirling wheel, rising up from the horizon and reaching high into the dark sky. It was in the distance, out of our reach, but it shed enough light to illuminate our path through the heavy rainfall. No words can describe it, as I have seen nothing like it before or since. It was simply out of this world. I became tongue-tied and my mind swiftly glided into ecstasy as I saw this illumination reach the sky from the horizon. I stopped walking for the first time that night. Completely forgetting about everything, I shouted out loud:

"Do you see it? Do you see it?"

"I see it, I see it clearly!!"

"Yes, yes, I see it too!!!" The two women were also beside themselves.

We did not say anything else or think about anything else. We simply followed the light. I have no way of knowing how far we walked toward that pillar of fire. We walked and walked like mad zombies. Soon there appeared another two rows of barbed-wire fence, and we jumped over them without thinking. We were simply marching toward the incredible magnet. It felt like I was living in one of those biblical miracles, like when Moses opened a path in the Red Sea for his people to escape. The pillar reminded me of Jacob's ladder connecting earth to heaven. The pillar of fire, which was guiding our movements, was not of this world. It was God's providence.

We did not know where exactly we were heading. All we knew was that we were following the guiding light. We were in complete oblivion when harsh flashlights brought us back to this world.

A border guard was yelling at us in an incomprehensible language, but it was obvious he was ordering us to halt. We stopped, gradually coming to our senses and realizing that we had been discovered. It was still pouring. There was no more pillar, but we saw flickering lights in the distance, which looked like a compound of two or three barracks. Still mesmerized by what we'd seen, we did not resist but followed the guard to the border station. When we entered, we were completely shocked. We were in China! We saw the red flag with yellow stars on the wall and froze. We looked at one another in fear. The divine guiding light had led us to dangerous territory! We had walked all night without a break and we were still in China! The Chinese guards made us take off most of our clothes and started searching every single inch of our possessions. One guard even ripped off all three backpacks, including the padded straps, to see if we possessed any contraband. Our backpacks and the personal belongings inside them were completely soaked, but the Chinese kept scrutinizing every little detail. I was extremely afraid because I was carrying a map of China in the back pocket of my jeans. Mrs. M had given it to me in Yanji after she marked all the cities that we'd stayed in or were going to pass, which exposed the trail of our escape from the Korean-Chinese towns of Tumen and Yanji to Beijing, then to Erenhot, and finally to Mongolia. If the guards saw the map, there would be little question where we'd come from or what we were trying to do. I was scared to death. I held my breath as I silently watched how the search progressed. The other two were also in silent panic. The patrol examined all the belongings that Mr. and Mrs. M had given us upon our departure: shoes, South Korean passports, underwear, toothbrushes and skin lotion, towels, Bible, first aid kit, pen, and notebooks. My jeans, which were completely soaked by the rain, were thrown on one of the chairs and not scrutinized. I held my breath to conceal any signs of anxiety and watched how raindrops dripped down the windowpane one after another, first at short intervals, then at more prolonged intervals, waiting until the guards finally searched the jeans. However, miraculously enough, they completely neglected to check them. After the thorough search, they returned our belongings and let us change into new clothes from the backpacks. L was as relieved as I, since she was carrying her North Korean Workers' Party membership card. She held onto it for the day she had to prove who she was back in North Korea. However, in this particular situation, it would have really harmed everyone. Having anticipated the danger of being exposed before she reached the final destination, when we left Yanji, she decided to keep it safely in the most secretive place in her body. When the police left us to change our clothes, she whispered how glad she was to have rolled the membership card, wrapped it in plastic, and inserted it in her vagina.

On the Threshold

At first we were detained in the garage. We decided that we would act as if we were South Korean tourists who'd gotten lost during a tour of the border region. We agreed to argue that we'd voluntarily come to the patrol station to seek help. We protested with all our might, banging the metal door with our fists and shouting.

"How can a socialist country lock up people who came to seek help from it?"

The Chinese guards, not understanding a word of Korean we spoke, would respond by banging the door with their metal club. This noisy back-and-forth went on for a while. A couple of days later, we were transferred to a medical ward with ten hospital beds. Two armed guards were on duty outside. We got scared. We would end up in North Korea and die if we did nothing, so we decided to go on a hunger strike and demand that we be sent back to Mongolia where we'd come from. We started fasting and kept praying. L prayed most fervently throughout the entire period. She used to read palms and tell fortunes in North Korea, but she had turned into an ardent believer of Christianity. With L leading the prayers, we fasted for fourteen days at that border station, drinking only water. By the end of the last day we were so weak that we almost crawled, dragging each other, to go to the toilet. The Chinese authorities became worried that we would pass out under their supervision. Now they were guarding us not because they thought we would escape, but because we might faint and require medical attention at any moment. They started bringing in more delicious food, but we would not touch any. The commander of the post would come and talk to us. He was a skinny, scruffy man in his mid-fifties, always smelling of alcohol. The last time he came to see us, he brought porridge and told us many things, which were all communicated through body language without an interpreter. He said that he believed we were South Koreans, but in order to prove that we really were, we had to give up fasting and regain strength. He told us more strange things, and I do not understand to this day why. God lets things happen through human agency in the most unexpected ways. The commander told us that thirty miles directly north of the post was a border region between China and Mongolia without any physical demarcation line. But it was a dangerous route since there were wild foxes waiting for human prey, so he would not recommend it. Even more surprisingly, he told us that it would be better for us to try the wire dividing the two countries. Through vivid body language, he told us we need to bend at the waist to keep from being seen by the night watch's binoculars when walking around this area. He said that in a couple of days he would be away for three days' training and told us to be well in the meantime. Then he once again offered us the porridge and left. We followed his advice and ate it all. We were amazed by how much he'd told us and took it as a message that if we were planning to escape, he wanted us to do it during his absence. It was also amazing that we could communicate with one another by using limited Russian vocabulary and body language.

L told me that she had a premonition that the guards would hand us over to the immigration authorities in Beijing since they'd had us in custody for too long. Being sent back to Beijing meant death, because even if we ended up in the South Korean embassy, the South Koreans would soon find out that our passports were fake and would not do anything to help us. The embassy in Beijing simply did not want to upset China, and accepting North Korean refugees against Chinese intention to repatriate them was not in their interest. Even worse, if we were handed over to the North Korean embassy, we would surely be sent back to North Korea for execution. We gathered our wits to plan for escape. We noticed that after we'd started fasting, the guards became inattentive, as they knew that we did not have the strength to run away. They would often doze off late at night. A few days after the meeting with the commander, we escaped, having realized that the guards fell asleep immediately after they arrived at their post. The strange commander was still away for training. At 2:00 a.m. we grabbed the chance and removed a mosquito net from a small ventilation window. There was really no way to pack anything except for money and passports; we left everything else behind. Instead of wearing shoes, we wore three layers of socks in order to make a silent exit. I helped the two women escape first through the window. I have heard that people can summon superhuman power when they face extraordinary circumstances determining life and death, and I went through amazing moments of survival myself when escaping from camp. But when I saw those two famished women fly out of that high window, I could not help but be reminded of the extraordinary power that is innate in every human being. Completely enervated from the prolonged hunger strike, they were literally dragging each other to the toilet just a few hours before! I also do not remember how I crawled out that small window. We lowered our torsos as the commander had told us to do and started to run away from the brightly lit area surrounding the post. Mongolia was just steps away beyond the multiple layers of barbed wire. We ran about a mile and a half until we ran into the barbed-wire zone. The women's shirts got stuck in the fence and we had to pull or drag one another. Our arms and legs were scratched and soon covered with multiple cuts. Nevertheless, we were running for our lives and nothing could stop us. We heard barking dogs and saw flashlights behind us as we were finally crossing the border. Our feeble, famished bodies were covered with sweat and blood, and all three of us lost consciousness soon after setting foot in Mongolia.

The Journey Continues

A tingling sensation of water drops rolled down my cheeks. When I opened my eyes, I saw the broad face of a stern-looking middle-aged man. I was lying on the ground, surrounded by an entire platoon of Mongolian border guards looking down at us. The stern-faced man was their leader. He was sitting on a stool and sprinkling water on us with a long willow branch that he dipped into a bucket of water. The two women were still unconscious. We looked like fugitives, without shoes and with torn clothes stuck to our bloody skin. I worried that the Chinese might have informed their Mongolian partners about our escape. When the two women woke up, the platoon leader brought an interpreter to interrogate us. He was a young Mongolian man who had spent a year studying the Korean language in Seoul.

"Where are you from?" he asked in clumsy Korean.

"We are from Seoul," I answered.

"Which part of Seoul are you from?" he asked.

We were dumbfounded. None of us had ever been to Seoul.

"We live near the South Gate area." I finally pulled out an answer.

"South Gate area?" The man paused for a second and then came up with another question. "What kind of cigarette do you smoke?"

"TC," I answered immediately, recalling the only South Korean cigarette brand I knew. As the Seoul Olympics approached in 1988, the South Korean government had sent TC cigarette packages to North Korea, dangling from helium balloons. However, that had been more than a decade ago and I had no idea if they were what South Koreans smoked nowadays.

"Can you name some other South Korean cigarette brands?" The man kept pounding me.

"Well, I really don't care about the South Korean brands. I am fond of Japanese cigarettes and mostly smoke Mild Seven."

"Can you name some of the bridges over the Han River in Seoul?" he turned to the two women and asked. There was no way we could answer that question, so they kept silent.

The interpreter started talking to the Mongolian authorities in a language completely incomprehensible to us. Even though I did not understand a word of it, I could sense that the interpreter did not believe we were from Seoul. After the conversation, the authorities detained us for two days. We were in a city called Dzamyn Üüd, not far from Erenhot. The Mongolian authorities put us in a dark basement cell. We were nervous, as our journey had gotten derailed from the original plan. Hadn't Mr. and Mrs. M told us that everything would be all right once we reached Mongolia? At this point, nothing looked certain. On the third day, they handcuffed us and ordered us to get on a truck. Besides the three of us, there were two Chinese illegal border crossers. They also had their hands cuffed, and they were blindfolded. As our eyes were not covered, I could see that they were taking us to the legal passage between the Chinese and the Mongolian borders. A straight white line divided two rows of barbed-wire fence. On each side, the Chinese and Mongolian national flags were hanging. Two Mongolian border guards got out of the truck and met two Chinese guards. They stood on each side of the white line and started having a heated discussion. From the truck I could hear a Chinese guard saying, "*Bu xing*," which I knew meant "no good," to his Mongolian counterpart. The arguing went on for about half an hour. Then a jeep arrived from the Chinese side of the border and a familiar face appeared in front of us. It was that strange Chinese commander who had voluntarily told us information when we were on the Chinese side. He still looked boozed up. I could see that he was explaining to the Mongolians through an interpreter that we'd originally walked into Chinese territory from Mongolia by accident, which was why we ran back to Mongolia. So the Mongolians should decide what to do with us—whether to hand us over to the South Korean embassy or the North Korean embassy.

The Mongolian negotiator was a rough man, resembling a wild boar. He would not cave in and threatened that they would not return the two blindfolded Chinese men if the Chinese were to reject us. The negotiation failed, and all five illegal border crossers were sent back to the Mongolian post. We were detained another week, the three of us in the same room. The Mongolian police gave us nothing but a blanket for each. They brought us soup and bread, which were hard to touch because of the pungent smell. Whenever the police saw us not eating, they gladly took the food and ate it in a split second. The Chinese police had never touched the food we refused, but the Mongolian soldiers were desperate. I could not understand why the Mongolians blindfolded us and dragged us when we wanted to go to the toilet as if sending a convict to the execution ground. There were neither walls nor doors in the toilet, so the guards could see us taking care of our very basic needs.

After spending a week in these primitive conditions in fearful uncertainty, we repeated the same routine. The three of us and the two Chinese border crossers were again brought to the passage between China and Mongolia. The Chinese and Mongolian authorities started arguing again. Then, in half an hour, the Mongolians, with angry faces, ordered us to get off the truck. It looked like the negotiations had failed. My heart sank. We would be sent back to Beijing! This was a nightmarish scenario.

As soon as we got down, the Mongolians freed our cuffed hands.

"Kim!" The Mongolian guard shouted out my name.

Two guards took my arms and escorted me. They started to walk like robots in ridiculously measured steps, dragging me to the white borderline and stopping there. Two Chinese soldiers approached in equally ridiculous steps, ready to receive the transferred illegal border crossers. The Mongolians pushed my back, and in a second I was in Chinese territory. The world went completely black and I could not see a thing as the Chinese soldiers dragged me to a truck, tightly holding my arms. My heart nearly stopped at that moment. All the risks I'd taken, all the risks my friends had taken, all my benefactors' efforts to save me from danger—it all came to a silly end like this. . . . The Chinese guards ordered me to get into the open back of the truck. It reminded me of the moment when I was arrested at the port of Nampo in North Korea. I came back to my senses only when the jolly Chinese truck driver started to offer me watermelon in an incomprehensible language. I looked around the truck and saw the belongings—shoes and backpacks—we'd left behind at the Chinese post. Seeing those things, I was even more assured that the Chinese were going to send us directly to Beijing.

"L!" the Mongolian guard shouted. The same ridiculously measured steps transferred her to the Chinese side and brought her to the truck. The chatty truck driver offered her watermelon. When the third member of our group was in the truck, the Chinese guards started yelling at us to get out of the truck again. When I got out, they yelled at me, pointing at my backpack and shoes. We were dumbfounded, but they kept yelling at us to pick up our packs and shoes. We obeyed. Since the straps of the packs had been ripped off, we held our stuff in our arms. The Chinese brought us back to the white demarcation line. None of us could figure out what was going on. Now, on the Mongolian side, there were the two Chinese illegal border crossers with blindfolds on. The Chinese guards pushed me to the Mongolian side and received one of the blindfolded men, after which each side signed some documents. Then the Chinese handed over L and received the other blindfolded Chinese. Again legal documents were signed in exchange. Then the Chinese finally sent the last in our group. It turned out that the Mongolians had lost their argument with the Chinese and had to accept that we'd originally crossed the border to the Chinese side by accident and had run back to Mongolia. Since the Mongolians had caught us running away from China, they first had to hand us over to the Chinese authorities, who would then legally hand us over to Mongolia. That was the entire charade we were subject to, but we did not know it then.

That was not the end of our border ordeal. The Mongolians took us back to the post and ordered us to strip down. There was no segregating men from women, and the three of us stood completely naked in front of the authorities. The medical inspectors came in to see whether we had any visible signs of disease, even looking into our rectums. L was particularly nervous about her North Korean Workers' Party membership card. After the inspection, they left us. We were locked up again but this time, we had all our belongings back from the Chinese authorities. They did not take away anything and every personal item we'd received from Mr. and Mrs. M was intact.

Now that we were in safe territory, we had to recuperate our strength. We did not know what the Mongolian authorities were planning to do with us, but we knew that we still had not reached our final destination. We asked the guards to buy us decent food and expensive cigarettes. They complied because they could get something out of us each time they ran errands. The two women once again demonstrated superhuman power when they ate everything with mighty appetites. However, having gone through tremendous fear and stress, I felt my blood pressure surging and felt nauseated. I lay down and could not get up when the police ordered me to. When it was clear that my illness was getting worse, the two women started yelling at the police.

"You savages, he is going to die if you don't take care of him! Savages!!!"

I did not know where these women got their tremendous vocal strength. The guard, who had been getting chubbier because of us, called his superior. They brought doctors to take my blood pressure and examined me with serious expressions on their faces. They were on the phone for a while, and it was decided that we would be transferred from Dzamyn Üüd, which was near the railroad, to Ulaanbaatar. Two security guards escorted the three of us. While the women were not restrained under their supervision, I was handcuffed and watched over by one of the two guards. When they put us on the train, I could clearly see for the first time the town where we had been detained. There were guards along the railroad tracks and not many regular houses to be seen. All the residents were families of either railroad workers or border guards. If we had ended up here as we'd planned, without going through the Chinese patrol station, we would have been caught immediately. I felt that God had planned it the way it happened, leading us on a safe path toward salvation. When we ended up in China, I could not understand how he'd led us to trouble instead of to a safe haven, but now I could. Only later did I learn that had we been caught by the Mongolian authorities, we would have been transferred to the Chinese authorities like the two Chinese illegal border crossers they exchanged for us. That would have surely meant our deportation to North Korea.

On the train, both women protested against handcuffing an ill person. The Mongolian guard released only one of my hands. Nevertheless, I felt a slight sense of relaxation. But at the post in Ulaanbaatar we were led to an unpleasant basement cell, which was dark and humid. Water dripped from the ceiling. There were no light bulbs, only candlelight. Everything was extremely primitive. On the other side of the wall I could hear a kind of murmur that sounded more like wounded beasts than human beings. We told the authorities that we were South Koreans and needed immediate medical attention. I was close to losing consciousness due to extreme high blood pressure. A female doctor came to check my blood pressure and noted that I was in a precarious condition and needed immediate care. After her visit, I noticed that about 6,000 Chinese *yuan* I'd been keeping in my pocket was missing. It could have been anyone who'd had close contact with me, but I suspected that it was the doctor. She was extremely kind and attentive, urging the authorities to move me to a better place. They put us in an upstairs office, where three beds were set up. The doctor brought a chloride injection and took good care of me, so I decided not to raise the issue of my missing money.

A few days after we'd moved upstairs, the Mongolian authorities called L to their office. She came back after a few minutes, completely pale. She could not open her mouth to explain what had happened but kept shivering as if struggling with a severe case of flu.

"North Korea . . . people from the North Korean embassy are here to see us . . . ah . . . my . . ."

It took a while for her to regain composure, but then she told us that the North Korean government was looking for that missing midcareer North Korean diplomat and his wife who had been stationed in Beijing. The NSA had issued their photos and was searching for them. When the North Koreans made the request to see us, the Mongolian authorities asked the South Korean embassy their opinion. I learned later that the South Korean intelligence in Mongolia by now had heard about my background from the missionary couple and wanted to protect me, so they told the Mongolian authorities to show only the women, not the man, as they were worried that someone from the NSA might recognize my face. So L was sent out for viewing. She told us that a black Mercedes sedan displaying a North Korean flag pulled over about three feet away. Nobody got out of the car, but someone lowered a backseat window and started to compare her face with the photo. They took their time and kept scrutinizing her. She was wearing fashionable glasses and a fancy black cashmere sweater with elegant white embroidery. Around her neck hung a gold chain and a gold cross, which she had received from Mrs. M. No matter how scared L might have been, she must have looked like anything but a North Korean escapee. The North Koreans kept looking at her for about fifteen minutes, during which time the Mongolian authorities kept pointing at L and repeating, "South Korean, South Korean." After the deadly inspection, the luxury sedan left L standing there, shaking. I thought about the possibility of an NSA agent inspecting me from the backseat of the car, had I been summoned. If, by any chance, the inspector had been a former colleague, would he have recognized me? I had changed so much since those happy days.

We spent two more days in the office. The female doctor brought us flowers, played music, and took great care of us. In hindsight, I guess I made the right choice of exchanging the money for good care and service, if she was the one who stole it. In the end, the Mongolian authorities took the rest of our money, nearly $4,500, as they charged us a huge sum for services they provided during our stay. The average monthly wage in Mongolia was $100 back then, so it was a large amount for them.

Soon after, a man who claimed that he was from the South Korean embassy showed up. We asked him for his ID, as we were not in a position to trust anyone yet. He showed us a diplomat's passport. L handed over her party membership card, on which her photo and Kim Il-sung's photo were displayed, as proof of the past she'd left behind. The man seemed surprised. He left the room and came back five hours later. He told us that there would be an interrogation by the Mongolian authorities and advised us to tell the entire truth, as he thought it was the best way to pursue political asylum. If we insisted that we were South Koreans, it would not help our situation, as the Mongolians did not really believe that. He promised to make arrangements for our safety. Next day, as the diplomat had indicated, the interrogation began. I told everything to an interpreter—about my imprisonment in the political camp, my escape, and my journey to China and Mongolia. Around 5 p.m. a high-ranking Mongolian official came in and talked to me through an interpreter:

"From a humanitarian stance, from now on I will treat you as a lieutenant colonel of the North Korean Army."

He asked all of us to get into his sedan and drove us around the city. The car passed the imposing North Korean embassy building in downtown Ulaanbaatar. We all held our breath and looked at the building in the dusk. Then the officer took us to a local grocery store and encouraged us to buy whatever we needed or wanted. I picked up a can of pickled garlic, cucumber, a pack of cigarettes, sauerkraut, and a bag of rice. He then paid for the groceries himself. It must have been with our money that had been taken away, but we could neither say anything nor care too much about it. Then he took us to a hotel in the city, where the manager came out to greet us in a stiff, ceremonious manner. The officer told the manager to take good care of us, as we were South Korean tourists in need of special assistance. The manager checked us into a large suite with two king-size beds and started sending room service whenever we needed it. This was truly a comfortable refuge compared to the border posts and cellars we'd been detained in for almost half a month.

The next day the South Korean diplomat came to see us. He told us that the Mongolian government would protect us until our departure and gave each of us $50, but he did not say where we would be sent. He told us to stay in the hotel area and not venture out for our own safety. When he left, we talked about whether to completely trust this South Korean. L had the phone number of a South Korean pastor in Ulaanbaatar. Mrs. M had given it to her in Yanji in case something happened in Mongolia. That night, she went down to the hotel lobby and called the pastor. He came to our hotel five minutes later. We shared our worries and concerns with him, and he replied that if we felt in danger, he could make us fake South Korean passports and smuggle us out of Mongolia on an express train to Moscow. But when he heard that the South Korean embassy was already involved, he was more relaxed. We could not believe that the same South Korean government could behave so differently in Beijing and here, but the pastor said we need not worry too much. A week passed, during which all kinds of thoughts came in and out of our minds. Then a Mongolian police officer came to see us and suddenly shook our hands in a congratulatory way.

"Kim Il-sen [Kim Il-sung]? No, no more North Korea. To Pyongyang."

He was telling us that the North Korean embassy in Ulaanbaatar was now closed down due to North Korea's financial difficulties.[1] We could not believe what he was saying. We had seen its massive building just a week ago. It had sent NSA people in a Mercedes to inspect L not too long before that. When the police officer saw our dumbfounded faces, he asked us to get in the car and drove us to a square downtown, at the corner of which stood the embassy building. Just as he'd told us, there was no longer a North Korean flag hanging by the gates. The displays of leaders' photos along the embassy walls had all been taken down. The officer said that from now on we did not have to be confined to the hotel and could go out into the city if we wanted.

The following three months in Mongolia was a joyful period, as we were provided with a safe place to stay and were assured by the South Korean embassy that we would reach our final destination soon. Every day we rode buses and visited tourist spots. The women bought cosmetics with their pocket money and urged me to buy a leather jacket in preparation for the cold winter. Every day was like a picnic. We also visited a restaurant called Arirang run by a South Korean owner. Two women told him that we were from North Korea. At first he could not hide his surprise, but having heard the story, he gave us his phone number and urged us to call him if there was any emergency. He then invited us to dine at his restaurant for free. He said he would even pack our breakfast and lunch if we wanted to eat elsewhere. We were the first North Korean refugees he'd ever encountered, and he generously provided kind assistance as he could. He owned a car and took us places whenever he had time. The Mongolian guards who were assigned to protect us also accompanied us. The pastor kept visiting us and we visited his church, becoming close friends.

In late December, when Ulaanbaatar was covered with harsh winter frost, we boarded a Korean Airlines plane bound for Seoul, Korea. All the people who had befriended us—the pastor, the owner of Arirang, the Mongolian guards—came to the airport to see us off. By then we had become close, like a family. They all wished us well and promised to let us know when they came to Korea. The two women cried and so did I, holding their hands tightly as the warmth of our hands communicated our feelings. When the plane took off, I saw the evening sun shining bright over the right wing outside my window. This was the sun I'd been dying to see for six years when I was working in the camp mines. It shone beautifully over the snowy city of Ulaanbaatar. That moment, I felt like part of myself was set free, beaming in the gleaming rays as I flew closer to my destination.

Afterword

UNFINISHED STORY

The first days in South Korea were marked by alterating excitement, relief, and exhaustion. I was immediately escorted to a heavy-security debriefing facility where many South Korean intelligence officers asked me an endless succession of questions—one after another. I told them everything. They paid attention to every detail and treated me with respect appropriate for my rank in the North Korean People's Army. Although I did not have to worry about imminent danger of being captured or sent back, I felt weary. I felt confined within the white walls of the modern facility, regularly served meals, and polite intelligence officers. Having been on the run and in hiding for almost one year, I found this settlement strangely unsettling. During this time, I seldom saw my two female fellow travelers, since we were being kept and debriefed in different offices. Since I came to South Korea with an experience uncommon among most defectors, my debriefing process was thorough and long, which kept me in isolation for the most part. The occasional break from this monotonous interim period was Ping-Pong matches, which let out my hidden passion for physical activities. The South Korean intelligence officers teamed up, and I joined another North Korean defector in a fiery match representing the two sides of Korea. The matches became so dead serious that they started to resemble hostile exchanges of gunfire across the DMZ. Sometimes, each side's determination to win became so strong that vitriolic comments were pronounced carelessly. At these moments, I was able to forget about my current reality of being a North Korean defector in a South Korean intelligence facility. At least during these heated matches, I was again a boy athlete in Mansudae Children's Palace competing feverishly for the glory of the Great Leader and our fatherland.

What seemed like an eternity at the facility also came to an end, and then came the reeducation period at Hanawon—a facility that provided North Korean defectors with a crash course on the details of South Korean life. Brief overviews of the geography and history, the banking system, the basic social skills, and such were taught. There I met North Koreans from all walks of life and learned the details of the hardship and danger they'd endured in reaching this place. Many of them had left family and friends behind in the north, and this weighed heavily on their hearts and minds. Although they were on the brink of starting a new life in the south, many were steeped in memories of the past, haunting them with nightmares in which they were illegal border crossers again and their bodies hung on the gallows in public as a display to inspire horror. Other times, the past returned wearing the faces of their loved ones, pleading to be taken away from North Korea. This was the worst form of nightmare for many, evoking guilt that was more tormenting than physical pain. The haunting memories of their families dragged them back to the abyss of the past, which loomed dark in the face of the present, entirely eclipsing visions of the future ahead of them.

Soon after my release from Hanawon into South Korean society, I came upon a question with which I had to wrestle for a while. The Christian community in South Korea was extremely active in assisting North Korean refugees, not only those still in danger after their escape and before they reached a safe haven but also those who had difficulty settling in South Korea, which was so different from the place they'd left behind. Had it not been for the helping hands of these Christians, God knows what might have happened to me in China. Had they not hid me in safe places there and taken care of me with all their might, I would have found no means to make it this far. I felt forever in debt for their humane and selfless devotion, but it did not automatically compel me to become a believer. After all, I'd spent most my life in a place where Christianity was known to be a poisonous element paralyzing people's minds. An idea of the religion as a deceptive means to exploit naïve believers was instilled over and over again in North Korea. How could I suddenly fall in love with it, even though I owed my life to Christians I'd met in China? South Korean Christian community workers helped me as much as they could, taking me to their church so that I could be plugged into a community of friends and newly arrived people from the north. They also wanted me to enroll in a Christian university that would prepare me to become a pastor. When these friends at church sent an application form to my home address, I tore it up, not wanting to be forced into something I still had doubts about. Then came another application and I tore it up as well. When the third one came, I finally succumbed to the strong-willed friends who wanted me to go down the same path as they had—to set out on an altruistic mission to save the less fortunate. I thought I'd give it a try.

It wasn't long after I enrolled in the university that I revisited the unbelievable vision I'd seen in the Gobi Desert. The pillar of fire that had illuminated our path in the thick of the night started to enrapture me and haunt me with questions. Was it the divine providence that turned doubters into men of God? Did Abraham and doubting Thomas see the same vision before they professed their eternal faith in God? When my co-travelers and I saw the pillar that night, we had no doubt that it was not from this world. It was from God and God alone, as a manifestation of his grace leading lost souls to the road toward salvation. But why would he love me, the one who used to deny his presence, who used to doubt his words, even when Mrs. M in China urged me to take his words to my heart and pray? Had he designed a test for me similar to the one he gave Job?

Although there were many helping hands, my first days in South Korea were not easy by any means. Whenever opportunities arose, I spoke openly about how my human rights were abused in the North Korean camps. I also granted interviews with various media to publicize the state-sponsored atrocities in North Korea. No too long after, I started to receive strange phone calls. The man on the other end never identified himself, but he admonished me not to speak of the North Korean camps and hung up. I was frightened. I remember the moment when I'd signed the document not to divulge anything about my experience at Camp No. 14 before being transferred to Camp No. 18. Was the caller directly related to the North Korean NSA? Who was this mysterious person? Regardless of the caller's identity, one thing was clear: I was being watched closely by someone, which made me wake up at night with a reason to fear. However,

I could not live in forced silence after having gone through so much to reach this place. There must be a reason I'd come this far. My life had been in the mouth of death not too long ago, and I had to make a sense of my survival. On behalf of those thousands of North Korean prisoners who perished in silence, I simply had to bear witness.

Another big concern, naturally, was how to make a living. I was obviously not able to use my skills as a military officer earning foreign currency, so with the settlement funding that the South Korean government allocated to defectors from the north, I opened a North Korean noodle shop with a couple of friends who also felt lost in the market economy that was brand new to us. Although I recovered my health to the point that I could get by without noticeable physical discomfort, my face still revealed the scars and pains of the harsh days in the camp when I could not see the sun. My business partners joked that if I were to roam around in the dining area and serve customers, everyone would be terrorized and never come back again. Although they meant it to be funny, I read their minds and gladly retreated to the kitchen area where I could supervise noodle making. The business boomed at first, as shops like ours serving North Korean cuisine were rare, but this initial success soon turned into a problem. The jealous restaurant owner next door started to sabotage our business in numerous annoying ways, which culminated in cutting off our power line. While fighting all of these obstacles and trying to make a living, I was enrolled at the Christian university, taking a full load of classes when I was not shopping or cooking for the restaurant. I was in a permanent state of exhaustion, but it was nothing compared to what I'd had to endure in North Korea. One time when I was driving from my class to the restaurant, I slipped into slumber and had a very minor collision with a taxi right in front of me. It was not a crash by any means, since the traffic was jammed and no car could speed to create a huge accident, but the two female passengers got out of the backseat with an expression of great suffering on their faces.

"Oh, what horror, oh, what pain!"

"I am sorry. Are you all right?"

"Oh my, what a mess. . . . I will need to have a close examination of my neck for sure."

"I am sorry. . . . I hope you'll be fine."

"We might need hospitalization in order to get a thorough checkup. This kind of trauma does not get noticed at the early stage. You have to monitor it carefully in the hospital."

At this point, I said what I really felt like saying.

"Female comrades, with your feeble minds, how could you ever survive a war if North Koreans were to invade South Korea?"

These women looked at me, startled, as they noticed my obvious North Korean accent and manner of speech, but they soon gained composure and continued with their complaint.

"Don't worry, we will be as resolute as possible if there's war. War is war, but for now, we need compensation money for our neck injury."

I was feeling that enough was enough when an invitation to visit the United States came through a Korean-American church organization. I was only too glad to let myself be taken to a new destination.

I'd begun to wonder, as soon as I learned about my father's true background, about America. It was a place that caused our family unfathomable tragedy. It was the country for which my father worked during the Korean War and yet it tore everyone apart, sent children far away from parents and husbands from their wives. Its army still occupied the southern half of the Korean peninsula. Nevertheless, I was growing more curious than angry. I wanted to see with my own eyes what America was like and what my father had worked for at the cost of unspeakable grief. In March 2003, I was on a plane for New York and thinking about my father. I remembered nothing of him, but I was heading to a country that might be able to tell me more about who he really was.1

As a rare witness to one of the most atrocious gulags ever in human history, I gave lectures everywhere I went: churches, universities, community events. The most memorable of them all was to testify before the Human Rights Committee of the U.S. Congress in April 2003. In Washington, D.C., I also helped intelligence officers identify the locations of the North Korean camps and the facilities manufacturing counterfeit foreign currency. I was not sure to what degree they were interested in my knowledge about these facilities, but it turned out that they were not really paying attention; three years later, they seemed to have realized the importance of this story and came back to me with follow-up questions.

The tour was supposed to end on the West Coast with lectures and meetings. Los Angeles was the final destination, where many Korean Americans greeted me. Three days after my arrival, a letter was delivered to me from a Jewish lawyer who took a special interest in my story. She had read about it in the English-language edition of *Monthly Chosun* (Wolgan joseon), which featured the gruesome details of my internment in Camp No. 14. She was willing to help me apply for political asylum in the United States. My original plan had been to go to Japan after my visit to the United States, because I was feeling increasingly unsafe in South Korea with those mysterious phone calls urging me not to talk about the North Korean camps. So I agreed to this offer, hoping that the U.S. government could provide me with a safe refuge.

Soon after settling down in Los Angeles, I enrolled in a seminary and began to lecture for various churches. As I tried to embrace the teachings of love and forgiveness, my life became meaningful. My South Korean friends who'd urged me to explore Christian ways of life would have been happy for me. I became active in the community of North Koreans and did my best to advocate for their safety and rights while waiting for my case to be resolved. Although a labor certificate was issued in December 2004, I am still waiting for word about the asylum case, which will guarantee my permanent legal status in the States. I was introduced to the director of Immigration and Naturalization Services while in Washington, D.C. and many friends are advocating for me, but I am still waiting to hear from the INS and make the United States my adoptive home.

After getting settled in Los Angeles, I was able to ask my former business partner—a Chinese expatriate who travels frequently between China and North Korea—to salvage some family photos and bring them out of North Korea. He picked up pictures from my wife's brother, who did not know where the rest of my family had ended up. The only thing my brother-in-law could say was that after my arrest, my family was rounded up and sent to a remote mountain area. When I think of their surprise, terror, and anguish when that took place, I sink into unfathomable despair. Where have all those years when we were living under the same roof as a family gone? I would be only too glad to give my life to relieve their pain. My children must have grown up to be unrecognizable strangers. They were only five and three when I saw them last. If I were to pass by them on the street, would I be able to tell who they were? Against all hope, against the cruelly indifferent stream of time, my memory reverts to that morning of 1993. It was an ordinary day—peaceful and quiet. For some reason, my wife hand-washed the Nissan bright and shiny, early that morning. I remember thanking her for it. My son had already gone to school, but my wife and daughter were still at home and saw me off in front of the house. Our white dog was wagging his tail as I drove the car past the alley. In my mind, they are forever living that day.

For some time now I have thought about how to end my story. I thought it could end with my improbable escape from the camp. That moment I crossed the border between the living and the dead, when mental anguish alone could have cut the thin thread of my life; that moment when I saw the reflection of my face under the moonlight in Go-on. That chilly rivulet under the bright moon captured the fearful face of the hunted, but at least it was the face of a man freed from bestial captivity. Although my life was in jeopardy from unspeakable hunger, the harrowing possibility of betrayal and capture, I was at least free at that moment.

Or my story could end with my arrival in South Korea or the United States, where I did not have to worry about imminent capture or imprisonment, but life continued to take me through unexpected routes and challenges. Should I find solace in the way I managed to survive so many deaths to tell my story? In my mind, both versions are missing something significant. Though my story illustrates a journey through the dark and bright sides of fate, it has not reached its conclusion yet.

Ideally, this story should end with a reunion with my children and wife whom I left behind in North Korea. Whenever and wherever that might take place, it would be a perfect event to end this book. Just as the waves of the Californian shores indifferently repeat their swaying motion, my journey keeps moving forward and backward, without ultimate direction. There is no end to my story, and I know well it has to do with home.

Home for me is a place where the memories of people so dear to me are enshrined.

I long to go back and rejoice at my birthplace, where I grew up and began my travels along the bumpy roads of life—a life marked by both happiness and tragedies. It is still home to me. And yet, that place reminiscent of great joy and terror is still far from sight. Until I set foot there again, the journey continues, forward and backward.

Notes

Introduction by Kim Suk-Young

1. Carter J. Eckert et al., *Korea Old and New: A History* (Seoul, Korea: Ilchongak Publishers and Korea Institute at Harvard University, 1990), 328–29.

2. Quoted in Don Oberdorfer, *Two Koreas* (Indianapolis: Basic Books, 1997), 7.

3. The past decade (1998–2008) might have been a digression from the hostile inter-Korean relationship, since South Korean policy toward North Korea changed significantly under the presidency of Kim Dae-jung (1998–2003), who introduced the so-called "Sunshine policy" (*haetpit jeongchaek*). Taking its concept from Aesop's fable about a contest between wind and sunshine to make a traveler voluntarily remove his coat, the new policy advocated open dialogue instead of military conflict, mutual understanding instead of mutual accusation between the two Koreas. Under this policy, South Korea actively took the lead in engaging North Korea. The following president, Roh Mu-hyeon (2003–2008), continued this engagement effort, and inter-Korean exchange grew in all sectors. However, the "Sunshine policy" also invited severe criticism of the South Korean government that it is unwilling to confront North Korea about human rights abuses and refugee issues for fear that it might cause the inter-Korean relationship to deteriorate.

4. Charles Armstrong explains in detail that the cultural conflict between the two Koreas was in large part the outcome of the ideological competition and rivalry between the Soviet Union and the United States, the occupiers of the north and south, to win the hearts and minds of the Korean people on both sides. See "The Cultural Cold War in Korea, 1945–1950," *Journal of Asian Studies* 62, no.1 (Feb. 2003): 71–99.

5. Bruce Cumings, *Korea's Place in the Sun* (New York: Norton, 1997), 225.

6. Helen-Louise Hunter, "Society and Its Environment," in *North Korea: A Country Study*, ed. Robert Worden, 270 (Washington, D.C.: The Library of Congress Research Division, forthcoming).

7. Hwang Pong Hyok and Kim Jong Ryol, *DPR Korea Tour* (Pyongyang: National Tourism Administration, 2002), 99.

8. A chapter on the North Korean economy in Marcus Noland's book *Avoiding the Apocalypse: The Future of the Two Koreas* (Washington, D.C.: Institute for International Economics, 2000), 59–142, features some aspects of the North Korean government's foreign currency–earning activities.

9. For a detailed account with recent examples of North Korea's illegal activities on the global stage, see Balbina Y. Hwang, "Curtailing North Korea's Illicit Activities," http://www.heritage.org/Research/AsiaandthePacific/bg1679.cfm#pgfId-1049475 (accessed September 23, 2008).

10. Hunter, "Society and Its Environment," 223.

11. Charles Armstrong, *The North Korean Revolution 1945–1950* (Ithaca, N.Y.: Cornell University Press, 2003), 72–73.

12. Hunter, "Society and Its Environment," 223.

13. Richard K. Carton, ed., *Forced Labor in the "People's Democracies"* (New York: Mid-European Studies Center, 1955), 8. Quoted in Philip F. Williams and Yenna Wu, *The Great Wall of Confinement: The Chinese Prison Camp Through Contemporary Fiction and Reportage* (Berkeley and Los Angeles: University of California Press, 2004), 37.

14. Williams and Yu, *The Great Wall of Confinement*, 37.

15. Williams and Yu, *The Great Wall of Confinement*, 41.

16. David Hawk, the author of *The Hidden Gulag: Exposing North Korea's Prison Camps*, translates the term as "political penal-labor colony" as opposed to "political-detention camp," "prison camp," or "concentration camp." *The Hidden Gulag: Exposing North Korea's Prison Camps* (Washington, D.C.: U.S. Committee for Human Rights in North Korea), 18.

17. Ibid., 24.

18. Hawk, *The Hidden Gulag*, 24.

19. Hawk, *The Hidden Gulag*, 24.

20. David Hawk argues that there are six *kwanlisos* currently in operation, four of which have been confirmed in Kim Yong's testimony. Hawk, *The Hidden Gulag*, 26.

21. Kang Cheol-hwan, who spent ten years of his childhood in the infamous prison camp No. 15 in Yodeok, South Hamgyeong province, also provides a detailed account of food deprivation that caused madness and near starvation, driving inmates to eat anything to survive, including snakes and roaches. Kang Chol-Hwan and Pierre Rigoulot, *The Aquariums of Pyongyang: Ten Years in the North Korean Gulag* (New York: Basic Books, 2001).

22. Oleg V. Khlevniuk, *The History of the Gulag: From Collectivization to the Great Terror* (New Haven: Yale University Press, 2004), 105.

23. Williams and Yu, *The Great Wall of Confinement*, 87.

24. Stephen Haggard and Marcus Noland, *Famine in North Korea: Markets, Aid, and Reform* (New York: Columbia University Press, 2007), 209.

25. Ibid.

26. *Failure to Protect: A Call for the UN Security Council to Act in North Korea* (Washington, D.C.: U.S. Committee for Human Rights in North Korea, 2006), 58.

27. There are numerous testimonies regarding the plight of North Korean refugee women forced into sexual slavery, of which the following report is just one example. See "Lifting the Veil: Getting the Refugees Out: Getting Our Message In: An Update on the Implementation of the North Korean Human Rights Act," Joint Hearing Before the Subcommittee on Africa, Global Human Rights and International Operations and the Subcommittee on Asia and the Pacific of the Committee on International Relations, House of Representatives, 109th Congress, 1st sess., October 27, 2005, 22–23; http://www.foreignaffairs.house.gov/archives/109/24202.pdf (accessed September 19, 2008).

1. Coming of Age

1. Kim Jeong-suk was Kim Il-sung's first wife and the birth mother of Kim Jong-il, the current leader of North Korea.

2. In Russian the word means "victory." Pobeda was one of the best Russian sedans available in North Korea in the 1950s and '60s.

3. One meter is slightly longer than a yard and equals about 3 feet 3.5 inches.

4. In Korean the word means "sea of blood," which is also a title of a well-known revolutionary opera and film.

5. Approximately 240 miles.

6. Mangyeongdae is a site North Koreans worship as the sacred birthplace of Kim Il-sung. It is canonized as a national treasure and countless people, including foreign visitors, pay tribute to this place, which is composed of a modest hut and a small courtyard.

7. Samjiyeon is a lake located on the top of Baekdu Mountain on the North Korean–Chinese border. Just like Mangyeongdae, it is worshiped as a sacred revolutionary site, since it is the place associated with the antirevolutionary fighter Kim Il-sung's 1945 victorious return to his homeland from Manchuria, where he was in exile during the Japanese colonial days. Also, in the official North Korean media, Baekdu Mountain is identified as the mythological birthplace of the current leader, Kim Jong-il.

2. Living for the Great Leader

1. Kim Chaek was one of Kim Il-sung's most trusted comrades from the days of their anti-Japanese efforts in Manchuria. He is canonized as one of the revered communist leaders in North Korea, so much so that a city was named after him.

2. North Korean residents cannot freely choose their place of residency. In order to move, they have to have permission from the state. Pyongyang is a highly desirable place to live, and the only way for provincial dwellers to move into the city is to marry natives of Pyongyang or land a job there, both of which need approval from the state.

3 500 kilograms is roughly 1100 pounds. 1 kilogram equals approximately 2.2 pounds.

4. Gang Geon was one of Kim Il-sung's assistants during the latter's anti-Japanese guerrilla movement.

5. Equivalent to National Security Police.

6. Equivalent to police forces. After 1998, the name of this unit was changed to People's Safety Agency (*Inmin boanseong*). David Hawk, *The Hidden Gulag: Exposing North Korea's Prison Camps* (Washington, D.C.: U.S. Committee for Human Rights in North Korea), 22.

7. "Don't" in Russian.

8. Literally means "uncle" in Korean, but can be used to refer to a grown-up man.

3. Downfall of a Model Citizen

1. The author, Kim Yong, was known under a different first name, S, in North Korea. After his arrival in South Korea, the author changed the S to Yong to mark the beginning of a new life.

5. Escape

1. According to the official rate, 500 *won* is a rough equivalent of 230 U.S. dollars. However, according to the black market exchange rate, the actual value of 500 *won* is significantly lower. Until December 2001, the North Korean government insisted upon an official exchange rate of 2.16 *won* to the dollar, supposedly based on Kim Jong-il's birthday, February 16.

2. During the interview, Kim Yong called this Chinese town "Yeongil," a Korean pronunciation for "Yanji."

3. Kim Yong remembers this town as "Domun," the Korean pronunciation of the Chinese "Tumen."

6. Across the Continent

1. However, in the early 2000s, the North Korean embassy in Ulaantataar resumed operation.

Afterword: Unfinished Story

1. After his arrival in the United States in 2003, Kim Yong sent the CIA a letter of inquiry about his father's involvement with the organization during the Korean War. On September 30, 2008, Kim received a letter from the CIA claiming that his request cannot be met even under the Freedom of Information Act (FOIA). Under the FOIA, federal agencies are generally required to disclose records requested in writing.